P9-BBV-642

The Art of Conversation:

Magic

Key

to

Personal

and

Social

Popularity

James A. Morris, Jr.

A FIRESIDE BOOK
Published by Simon & Schuster
New York London Toronto Sydney Tokyo Singapore

Library of Congress Cataloging-in-Publication Data

Morris, James A., 1933-
    The art of conversation.

    Reprint. Originally published: West Nyack,
N.Y.: Parker Pub. Co., © 1976.
    "A Fireside book."
    1. Conversation.   I. Title.
[BJ2121.M76 1986]   395'.59   86-13848
ISBN: 0-671-63275-2

What This Book Will Do For You

"I wish I had said. . ."
"Why didn't he promote me into the new job?"
"Why wasn't I invited to the party?"
"I could have made a better impression if. . ."

These silent thoughts cross everyone's mind now and again. That's only natural—we all want to do better, and we all feel we will do better if only we have a few hints to help us master the art of conversing in such an engaging manner that people feel drawn toward us.

That is why this book was written—to present the *magic keys* that assure that your conversation takes on a magnetic quality that will truly make you more attractive and appealing to the people you meet.

You are awake 16 hours a day—5,840 hours a year. You spend more of this time contacting other people than in any other single activity. How well you converse with these people is the magic key to whether your days will be pay-off days filled with personal and social popularity. Now your days will be enriched as you become familiar with the easy-to-grasp magic keys presented here and they become a part of your personality. You'll want to use these magic keys in every contact with other people: they are your personal roadmap to pay-off, artful conversation. Start using them and you'll find others showing greater interest in you and your ideas: your social life will become more vital, your business career more rewarding, your whole life more exciting.

HAVING THE "GIFT OF GAB" DOESN'T ASSURE SUCCESS

John Simmons, for example, always thought he had the

"gift of gab," but then he noticed that people often ignored him or walked away when he was in the middle of a sentence. The more people walked away, the harder John talked, and the more he drove people away. It was a vicious, discouraging cycle. One day when we were chatting, John asked my advice on how to solve his problem. "Perhaps your trouble isn't caused by what you say, but by how well you listen," I suggested. This led to an interesting half hour in which we analyzed John's problem. From our discussion came the five magic keys for artful listening that I've expanded and presented in Chapter Two. They worked wonders for John and can do the same for anyone, whether or not he or she has the "gift of gab."

GUIDES TO GETTING STARTED

Rob Friedlan had the opposite problem. "I'm so shy and unsure of myself that I never hold my own in conversation," he once admitted to me. Ron's feelings aren't unusual; I've known many people who felt that way at some time in their lives. It was by helping people like Ron that I discovered the way to hold your own lies in knowing how to get started. You want to be able to approach another person and initiate a conversation. When conversation slows down and quiet sets in, you want to be able to start things going again. There are some simple and easy-to-use magic keys that will do just this. You'll find them fully explained in Chapter One, "Easy Ways To Start Pay-Off Conversations."

COMMUNICATION BECOMES AUTOMATIC

Coming back to the statements at the beginning of this introduction to the art of holding pay-off conversations, remember the all-too-common statement, "I wish I had said. . ."? How often have we been frustrated by the inability to make our point—by our inability to explain our thoughts well enough that the other person completely grasps what we are saying? Chapter Three presents a way to insure that you'll rarely ever say again, "I wish I had said. . ." The magic key presented in the third chapter is a very useful one: it shows you how to combine simplicity with clarity so that you will automatically communicate clear thoughts and ideas.

MEETING STRANGERS BECOMES EASIER

Whenever two people meet for the first time, there's a sense of uneasiness. You know the feeling—a sense of awkwardness—once the "hellos" are over, there's silence. Then a lot of meaningless statements are made as both people spar with words, searching for common interests, for common ground where they can meet in enjoyable, productive conversation. You can make these occasions less painful and infinitely more rewarding by using the shortcut magic keys detailed in Chapter Four.

PERSONAL SENSES ARE SHARPENED

There are many simple magic keys that, when used properly, unlock your natural qualities and let them shine through. Because these qualities are natural to you, they surely will increase your social and personal popularity. The magic keys that do the unlocking include a way to develop a pinpoint sense of timing, a method of keeping listeners attentive, an ability to key into the climate of a conversation, and the easily developed ability of using your five senses to add sparkle to your conversation. You'll learn how to make these simple techniques a productive, popularity-boosting part of your personality by reading Chapters Five and Six.

YOU'LL EASILY BUILD AN EXCITING KNOWLEDGE RESERVOIR

"I never know what to say," is a complaint I hear from many people. How often have we seen people standing in groups with closed mouths and blank faces? They seem to be at a complete loss; you can almost read their minds thinking: "I don't know what to say." The key word in this statement is *"know."* It makes sense—you cannot talk about something that you don't *know* about. That's why Chapters Seven and Eight are so important; they tell you how to choose the kind and type of knowledge that'll best help you become a respected, animated and popular conversationalist.

"Wait a minute," you say. "Even after I've chosen the knowledge that'll serve me well, I still have to learn it. That's a long, hard job." Not so: learning can be fast and painless and a lot of fun if you go about it in a systematic and organized way. Chapters Seven and Eight detail the magic keys that let you acquire popularity-boosting knowledge in the easiest and most effective way.

YOUR BUSINESS MEETINGS WILL PAY OFF–YOUR SOCIAL GATHERINGS BECOME MORE REWARDING

I'm sure you have noticed how good conversationalists quickly feel at home when conversing with a group of people. These popular conversationalists subtly take command of the group, artfully blend the various personalities together and keep everybody stimulated. They skillfully fan the flames of the conversation so it doesn't die out. When I first became aware of these good conversationalists at work, I thought this ability would be hard to develop. Since then I've found that it is really quite simple to do. I've observed sought-after conversationalists for years, analyzed their methods and distilled my observations into the proven magic keys you'll quickly learn by reading Chapters Nine and Ten.

ASSURING THAT YOUR CONVERSATIONS WILL PAY OFF

Businessmen and athletes share many traits. Perhaps the most important trait could be best explained by a remark Ed Lamanski once made to me: "The secret of my success is the ability to zero in on the right target, then to concentrate only on that target until I hit it smack in the middle of the bullseye. That's the way to get winning results."

You know instinctively that Ed is right. How can anyone play to win, in sports or business or everyday living, unless he knows what target he wants to hit, what goal he wants to score? Sure, keep your eye on the ball—but more importantly, keep at least the corner of your eye on where you want the ball to go.

Yes, Ed has the right idea, "The secret of my success . . . zero in on the right target." Ed's secret is really a series of logical and simple magic keys that many have followed and have won for them success and popularity as a result. These keys are fully explained in Chapter Eleven.

FRIENDSHIPS . . . PERSUASIVE POWER . . . SUCCESS . . . POPULARITY

These and other pay-off rewards are within the grasp of anyone who just reachs out for them. It doesn't take a lifetime of practice to see results; personal growth begins on the very first day you decide to start conversing better.

All you need do is move effortlessly through this quick-reading book. It's written in a way that helps you put its magic key techniques to work immediately. You'll find yourself automatically applying its magic keys and reaping its benefits and rewards right from the first day. All you have to bring to your reading is a sincere desire to start conversing better.

What caused me to write this book? The fact that I've seen so many people who have never realized their full potential as a person. On the other hand, I've also been privileged to know many highly successful and respected individuals. The difference between these two ends of the spectrum isn't as great as most people think. Sure, people are different—yet everyone is the same in one very important way. Everyone has some outstanding talents and personal qualities. The most useful tool available to a person to express these abilities is the tool of conversation. It's perhaps the one single method of expression that has helped the greatest number of people achieve their potential and know a sense of personal happiness.

I wrote this book to present the methods and techniques that can help people succeed in their business and social lives. These straight-forward, easy-to-use techniques, in the form of magic keys, will help everyone develop the skills that make that most important tool—conversation—a tool that will pay off for them.

James A. Morris, Jr.

Contents

1

Easy Ways to Start Pay-Off Conversations

Being able to converse well is one of the most important assets you can own. It helps you work effectively with others, it helps build new friendships and strengthen old ones, and it adds interest and sparkle to your life by making you the type of person others like to meet and enjoy being with.

Yet despite all these personal benefits . . . and despite the thousands of conversations going on every second of every day, it's surprising how many people are poor or uninteresting conversationalists. There's no logical reason for this. Anyone can be a good conversationalist; it isn't hard . . . all you have to do is apply a few simple techniques that are easy to learn and easy to use. In fact, they're so easy to use that once you try these techniques, they'll quickly become an instinctive part of your personality.

THIS SURE-FIRE TECHNIQUE MAKES YOU WELCOME ANYWHERE

And what technique could be easier to use than this one?

When a person makes a remark similar to the following, be a listener and not a speaker:

> "Let me tell you what happened on the way to work today!"
>
> "Do you know what the boss said when I told him how the project worked out?"

The listening technique is a sure-fire winner for you in situations like these. The person who's talking would consider you a good conversationalist even if you did nothing more than smile, nod, and say one or two words at the right time. He'd think well of you because he's obviously bursting with talk and wants someone to listen to him.

It's a proven fact that being a good listener adds breadth to your life by making you welcome in almost any conversation, and it quickly becomes a natural part of your personality. Just use it a few times and you'll find yourself instinctively noting when someone wants to talk and is looking for a good listener.

On the other hand, when you're with people who are not bursting with talk, you can still play the good listener role. The secret is to encourage others to speak up by using one of these two techniques:

1. When you're with only one person, ask questions that start him talking.
2. When you're with a group, spark a discussion based on a subject that interests most of the others present.

FIVE QUESTION-ASKING IDEAS

When there are only two of you in a conversation, the easiest way to get the other fellow talking freely is to ask him questions. Here are five ideas I've used quite often to help get a discussion off to a good start, and to make it pleasurable and profitable to both myself and the other fellow.

Ask Questions . . .

. . . *that appeal to his interests.* "Sam tells me you're a football fan. I missed last Sunday's game, but I heard that the Packers got off some great plays. Did you watch the action on TV?"

. . . *that lead into discussing his hobby.* "I see you're using a Leica. Are you a photography buff like me?"

. . . *that gets him talking about his job.* "When we arrived at the party, I noticed you parking a car with an Electronics, Inc. parking sticker on it. I've got a lot of friends over there. Do you work in the production or the engineering end of the company?"

. . . *that compliment him in some way.* I like your new sport coat. May I ask where you bought it? I've been searching for a good men's store."

Don't ask questions . . .

. . . *that pry into his personal life.* Obviously, your instincts will warn you not to ask a direct question such as, "With two kids in college, the financial strain must be great. How do you manage it?" It's common sense to wait until the other fellow first signals a willingness to talk by making a comment such as, "Am I glad I planned for the kids' education." This remark is a door opener, it leaves you free to reply, "I've got two kids in grade school now, so I have to start planning for their college education. But I'm not sure how to go about it. Have you any hints you could pass on?"

Similarly, you'd never bluntly ask, "I've heard the taxes are steep where you live. How hard do they hit you?" But if you really want to know what someone's taxes are, you can easily get the information by creating your own door opener, as John Dixon did in a conversation with Eric Samuels:

John: "I hear you live in West Hills. That's a beautiful area; I've often admired it."

Eric: "Thanks. We enjoy it."

John: "In fact, my wife and I have often discussed buying a house up there."

Eric: "I'll be glad to let you know if I hear of any for sale. But be ready to pay some pretty stiff taxes."

John: "Yes, I've heard that the tax bite's large."

Eric: "You bet it is . . . I'm paying $2000 now, and there's talk that they'll go even higher next year."

In summary, you can play the good listener role—and reap the double benefits of learning something new while making yourself welcome—by asking questions that appeal to the interest, hobbies or job of the other fellow. Be tactful when asking about subjects that border on the personal. Use these five question-asking ideas in your next few conversations, and you'll be surprised how quickly they'll become a natural part of your personality and help you get conversations off to an information-filled, fun-filled start.

HOW TO SPARK GROUP CONVERSATIONS

Asking questions is a great conversation starter when there

are just two of you present. When you're with a group,
however, you'll have more success using a broader-based technique: Pick a topic that interests as many of the others as
possible and spark a discussion on that topic. While there are
many ways of doing this, these three are by far the easiest to
use:

Get them working together on solving a problem.

Here's how Jim Thompson used this technique not only to
spark a conversation but also to get information he needed for
his job. Jim, who is Advertising Manager for Industrial
Automatics, was at a sales meeting eating dinner with five of his
company's top salesmen. Normally the supper-time conversation would have been a combination of kidding and story
swapping, but Jim needed some information about current
customer attitudes for a new advertising campaign he was
working on. He decided to combine business with pleasure by
asking the others, "I know competition is getting rougher these
days, and I'd like to give you more advertising support. But first
I need to know what problems you're running into. Can you fill
me in?"

Discuss a hobby or interest
that the group has in common.

At the first fall meeting of the Foreman's Club, here's how
Frank Lowell sparked an enjoyable conversation:

Frank:	"Did I have fun fishing this summer . . . I never saw so many bluefish before, but the stripers disappeared."
Tom:	"They were around. In fact, I caught some forty pounders."
Frank:	"That's unusual. Most fellows I know caught plenty of blues, but no stripers. What's your secret?"
Tom:	"Simple. I know where they went. When the blues came into the Sound this summer, the stripers moved from the Long Island side over to the Connecticut shore. I just followed them over."

Talk about a spectator experience you've shared together.

Assume you just attended a football game, and you're at a reunion dinner afterwards with some fellow college alumni. Since you're the only person who hasn't seen at least one other game, you have a perfect chance to relax and enjoy playing the good listener role:

> **You:** "What a pleasure today's game was to watch; the Lehigh team had spirit and they played hard even when the breaks went against them."
>
> **Gary:** "They've been that way all year . . . you should have seen the Delaware game. We did everything right, even pushed them back over their own goal line."
>
> **You:** "One thing confuses me . . . I had heard that Lehigh had a good passing offensive, but today they played a ground game."
>
> **Andy:** "That's because we used a different quarterback."
>
> **Bruce:** "Our regular quarterback got hurt last week, so we had to use our second string man today."

As you can clearly see, it's easy to start group conversations simply by getting others talking about a topic everyone finds interesting. It doesn't really matter which of the suggested techniques you use . . . whether you lead them into solving a problem, discussing a hobby or talking about a shared experience . . . any of these will work well for you. All you have to do is speak long enough to get the conversation under way. You can then sit back, listen and let the others do the talking. Use this approach for a while and it'll soon become instinctive. More importantly, people will quickly realize that when you're around, good conversations start. You'll be welcome wherever you go.

REACTIONS THAT
BUILD YOUR POPULARITY

It's almost uncanny the way people spot how you feel about them—and you can bet your last dollar that they'll react to your feelings . . . show friendliness and they'll return it . . . but if you take a dislike to someone, he'll surely spot it and immediately dislike you in turn. That's why popular conversationalists always think well about other people . . . they know that their positive attitude will be spotted and returned in kind. I've been watching popular conversationalists in action for quite some time, and I've discovered that they unconsciously use four basic techniques to assure their popularity.

Here's the best way to respond to others

Unless you're a hermit, there's no way to avoid contacting other people every day; and the way you handle these contacts is the key to whether you'll enjoy them or not. Here's an example of a very common way you can contact others:

- You can bury your thoughts and feelings deep inside yourself, put on a smile and act pleasant. Next you can get together only with others who also hide within themselves. Then everyone can stand comfortably at a safe distance from each other and bounce meaningless words off each other's shell. Some people call this conversation . . . but I call it a waste of time.

Just bouncing words off people is a shallow way to live . . . it's like eating the core of an apple and throwing the fruit away.

Try a more rewarding approach: Don't just bounce words around, but respond to everyone's uniqueness as a person. The easiest way to do this is by giving others your full attention, by putting their feelings and their thoughts ahead of your own. Do this for a while and you'll soon automatically ask yourself questions such as:

- "What kind of personality does my conversational companion have?" You can quickly spot this by simply observing how he speaks ... is he confident or hesitant, reserved or outgoing, self-impressed or down to earth?

- "What's his general attitude?" You can quickly spot this by noting if he's an optimist or a pessimist ... liberal or conservative ... and whether he willingly accepts newcomers to a group or is clannish and aloof.
- "When a new idea comes into the conversation, is his first reaction positive or negative?"

Questions like these will quickly arm you with workable insights into other people. You'll find it easy to respond and speak to each new person in a way he'll understand. More importantly, you'll show through actions and words that you recognize and respect each person's uniqueness. Do this and he'll surely respect and like you as a person in return.

The secret to being interesting.

When you want to be sure that you'll create a positive impression in the other fellow's mind, discuss a topic that interests him, not one that interests you. True, you may have to converse on topics that are boring to you ... but the time you spend in such discussions is a good investment, paying off handsomely in the long run. Take the example of John Watson, a sales manager, talking with one of his company's senior engineers. The engineer has just solved a rough technical problem; naturally he's enthusiastic about his breakthrough and wants to discuss it in detail. Now odds are that John Watson isn't the least bit interested in how the engineer solved his problem, but fifteen minutes spent sincerely listening to the engineer's story would pay off handsomely for John by winning his good will. If a customer later throws a tough application at John, you can be sure he'll have a good chance of getting the engineer to help him solve it.

You don't have to spend large blocks of time discussing topics that interest others; short ten- or fifteen-minute sessions are long enough. The important point is to get involved in enough of them so that other people think you are an interesting conversationalist, and this will surely happen as long as you keep steering your thoughts away from yourself and towards the other fellow's interests.

How to be sure you'll be tops in his book.

By applying your newly learned skills of recognizing the other fellow's uniqueness and discussing topics that interest him, you'll be well on the way to developing the positive attitude that will surely make you a popular and productive conversationalist. Another way to guarantee that you'll be accepted by others is to put their inner needs first. Here are two examples of how Joe Hardy does this:

- During one Monday morning coffee break, both Joe Hardy and Sam Goodrich were anxious to tell about their weekend golf games. Joe was particularly proud of his good score, but before he started talking, he first observed Sam. He knew Sam's game had been off lately, yet this morning Sam seemed anxious to talk . . . he must have had a change of luck. So Joe ignored his own desire to talk and let Sam brag about his good score. While Joe mentioned a few of his more interesting shots in passing, he made certain Sam remained front and center on the conversational stage.

- Joe arrived at a Friday night party thinking to himself, "At last it's the weekend. I'm going to relax, let loose and enjoy myself. I've earned it this week." Then he saw John Stretch approaching him, wearing a long face. Joe knew instinctively that John felt low and needed someone to listen to his troubles. He had a choice of either turning his back on John and joining the merrymakers across the room, or proving his friendship and earning John's good will by putting his own needs second and providing a sympathetic ear. Naturally, Joe chose to listen to John.

Wise conversationalists like Joe Hardy know that responding to the inner needs of the other fellow . . . and putting their own needs second . . . assures that they will be accepted in a conversation.

Helping the other person get his idea across.

Many people have trouble clearly expressing what's on their minds, and you can spot them easily . . . they'll fumble for words, keep repeating the same thought, act hesitantly, or otherwise give you the intuitive feeling that they're having a hard time communicating. When you spot such a person, you can help him by:

- listening creatively so you catch the basic thought he's trying to communicate
- and then helping him express himself clearly and accurately.

For example, suppose after taking dictation, your secretary hesitates before leaving your office, moves uncomfortably in her chair and then asks, "Is there anything I can do to help you?" You absentmindedly start to answer "no," but you stop yourself . . . there's an undertone in her voice that leads you to ask, "How's everything going back at your desk? Any problems?"

"Just fine, no problems at all. I was just wondering if there was any way I could be of help." The too-fast way she answers confirms your guess that she's not saying what's really on her mind. So you remark, "The best way you can help is by continuing to do the great job you are doing now. You're certainly taking a lot of detail off my back."

"I try. But if there is anyway I can improve, please let me know." That was the final clue you needed. "Hey," you say with a laugh, "I hope I haven't given you the wrong impression these past few weeks, but I've been so busy with special projects that I haven't been my usual self."

"Well, I was just wondering . . ."

Now that her concern over her performance is out in the open, your conversational path is clear. All you have to do is to assure her that she has done nothing wrong. Once this is done, you'll not only have solved a problem, but you'll have earned the loyalty of your secretary. After all, how often does someone take the time to help another person express thoughts that he's hesitant to voice directly.

HOW YOU CAN RISE ABOVE
COMMON HANGUPS

All through their lives many people fail to live up to their full potential as conversationalists. In fact, they actually hold themselves down, not because they lack the ability to converse, but simply because they lack faith in themselves: They don't believe they can hold a good conversation. This is nonsense; anyone can converse well.

As you think, so you are . . . no fact was ever truer. The way you think about yourself and the amount of belief you have in yourself are the factors that set the whole tone of your personality. Whenever you see someone holding himself down, you can be sure that his way of thinking is his own worst enemy. There's no need for this; anyone can turn his thinking in the right direction. There are techniques that anyone can use to rise above the common hangups that prevent him from enjoying the full pleasure and rewards of stimulating conversation.

Getting the best of timidity

Timid Toms become afraid and flinch away whenever they have to make a decision or take action on their own.

To rise above timidity, one must stop fearing the unknown. There's no way anyone can escape from facing unfamiliar situations. Life moves so fast today that it's impossible to live normally without running into new problems. So why not face up to this fact? Other people do everyday . . .

• A problem comes up on the job and Tim Long's boss calls him into his office. The boss needs his suggestions on how to solve the problem. Tim knows he'll score big with his boss if he forgets about his own personal timidity and thinks about the problem itself. By using common sense and applying logic and experience to the problem, he comes up with an answer. If you were in Tim's shoes, you'd be surprised at some of the answers you would be able to come up with in the same situation. It doesn't take a genius to solve a problem . . . most times all that's needed is a little old-fashioned horse sense.

- When Ron Cross entered his English class, he found his teacher asking questions about last night's homework. "This isn't the time to panic," he tells himself. "If I let timidity overcome me now, my marks will go into a sinking spell." Ron had read the assignment, so he forced himself to forget about his timidity and thought only about the questions. In a few short minutes he began speaking up and answering questions with the best of them.

The way to get the best of timidity is clear by now . . . just accept the fact that you have to face new and different situations every day and that you can't run away from them. Then when you face an unknown, think objectively about the problem and not subjectively about yourself. Do this and it won't be long before you'll stop tripping over your own timidity. You'll be surprised at how you'll unconsciously develop a sense of personal confidence, a new self-belief that will help you overcome any fears that pop up when you have to make decisions or take action on your own.

A technique that overcomes shyness

Many people are bashful and self-conscious . . . they're afraid to enter a conversation unless they know everyone in it, and they crawl into a shell whenever they meet someone new. Other people, however, overcome shyness every day. Salesmen call on new prospective buyers, teachers meet parents of children new to their class, and housewives run into friends while shopping and are introduced to accompanying strangers. Salesmen, teachers, housewives . . . yes, many of them are shy . . . but they don't let it get the best of them. They have learned one simple technique.

I call this technique the "round-about think." They simply

turn their thoughts 180 degrees away from themselves. They don't worry about how other people may react to what they say and do; rather, they think only about other people . . . what they are interested in, what they enjoy talking about, what conversational subjects spark their enthusiasm. As long as they keep thinking about the other fellow, it isn't long before they become completely engrossed in the conversation. They become so enthusiastic over what they're talking about that they completely forget their own shyness.

Why there's no need to shrink inside yourself

Some people I know are like ostriches . . . they poke their heads in the sand whenever they face a forceful personality.

It's easy to overcome this shrinking habit. First of all, accept the fact that you have weaknesses, and realize that it's uncomfortable when you're surrounded by others who are strong where you're weak. At the same time, accept the fact that you have strengths as well as weaknesses. Everyone has his own uniqueness. Accept these two simple facts and you'll clearly see that there's no logical reason to feel inferior. When you feel yourself being overawed by a strong personality, turn off your emotions and turn on your logic. Simply remember that you are a perfectly normal person with both strengths and weaknesses. You'll then be able to accept yourself, and you'll no longer feel the need to shrink from anyone.

Freeing yourself from inhibitions

Inhibited people form mental blocks that prevent them from talking casually with others. No matter how much they want to talk in a free and easy manner, something in their personality stops them when they try.

Inhibitions also can be easily overcome. The trick lies in how you choose what to talk about. Stick to topics where your interest and knowledge are very strong. Then you'll soon become enthusiastic about what you're discussing. Your enthusiasm will overpower your inhibitions and you'll talk freely. For example, if photography is your hobby, present a slide show to visiting friends . . . they'll enjoy hearing the story behind the pictures, and you'll enjoy telling each story. On the job, look for opportunities to help newcomers learn the ropes . . . they'll not only be grateful for your interest in them, but later on they'll return the favor by going out of their way to converse with you.

Don't worry about playing it safe

A play-it-safe person is extremely hard to talk with. Many businessmen are this way . . . they say little; and when they do speak, they measure every word as if they're afraid a bomb might go off if the wrong word pops out.

You can't go through life playing it safe . . . it robs your conversation of all the excitement and interest. So if you're this way on the job, stop being afraid of saying something wrong. A free-flowing graciousness and an honest interest in your fellow workers will certainly help you advance faster than a play-it-safe attitude will. Just stay clear of discussing sensitive topics where people's feelings run strong and your chances of saying something wrong will be almost nonexistent.

There's no need to be the group's wallflower

We all know someone whom we could call a "say-nothing person." This guy is quiet either because that's his natural personality or because he needs time to think about an idea before discussing it out loud.

It's easy to overcome this hangup. In a word, the technique is . . . enthusiasm. When you're in a conversation, shift your thinking into high gear and get excited about what's being discussed; then you'll automatically speak up and add to the conversation.

With the exception of the last item, each of these common hangups stem from the same root . . . fear. The easiest way to rise above fear is to steer your thinking away from your fears. As your thinking becomes more positive and constructive, your personality will automatically take on a new tone. You will develop the realistic and honest type of self-confidence that leads to successful and enjoyable conversations, and you'll be well on your way to becoming a pay-off conversationalist.

2

Five Steps That Make Your Listening Pay Off

Try this experiment: stop reading and close your eyes . . . imagine you're watching a discussion show on TV with the sound turned off but the picture kept on clear and sharp. Describe to yourself what your mind sees. This experiment illustrates the vital principle that in order for conversation to take place, there must be these two elements:

- Someone who delivers a verbal message, the speaker.
- Someone who receives the verbal message, the listener.

As you discovered when using your new skills learned in Chapter One, listening is as important in conversation as speaking. Now take a closer look at how you can make your listening skills even more rewarding and more productive.

OVERCOMING THE BARRIERS TO PRODUCTIVE LISTENING

There's really only one way to listen productively, and that's to remove all distractions from your mind so it's free to concentrate on the speaker. Nine out of ten times these distractions come from your thoughts, senses and emotions.

Controlling your thoughts

If you took a bottle and filled it with a quart of milk, the liquid inside the bottle would be pure and whole. But if you took the same bottle and filled it with a pint of milk and a pint of water, the liquid inside would be neither pure milk nor pure water.

Many people do much the same thing in conversation . . . they fill their minds with a pint of the message they're listening to and a pint of their own thoughts. When they do this, their mind is like the second bottle . . . containing neither the speaker's message nor their own thoughts, but a mixture of the two. You can learn from these people's mistakes . . . when someone is speaking, clear your mind of all personal thoughts and concentrate only on the speaker's words. This is sure to increase your listening productivity tenfold.

Sometimes a great new idea pops into your mind while you are listening to someone else; the idea is often important and you don't want to lose it. When this happens take a tip from my friend George Reade, a sought-after conversationalist. When George gets an idea, he doesn't fight the situation . . . he politely interrupts the speaker and asks him to bear with him for a few seconds while he writes down his idea. Then George's mind is free again to give his complete attention to the speaker. As George knows, once an idea is written down, you can safely put it out of your mind and enjoy the conversation . . . your idea will come back as soon as you read your notes at a later time.

Another very annoying distraction is the second-guessing game. Since you can think much faster than anyone can speak, it's often tempting to listen to the other fellow for a few minutes, then "second guess" what point he is leading up to. Some people even add a further insult: they interrupt the speaker and try to complete his thought for him. Although this may be good mental exercise, it's extremely poor human relations . . . the other fellow surely will leave the conversation with a very low estimate of your sincerity as a listener. Sought-after conversationalists listen attentively; only amateurs play the second-guessing game.

Controlling your senses

Consider how important conversation is to psychologists . . . it's the main working tool they have for helping people change their behavior. So it's only natural that these experts are always looking for more effective ways to converse. In one recent experiment, psychology students were told to conduct a series of five-minute counseling sessions using various approaches; all sessions were photographed and analyzed. The major finding: The best results were obtained when the trainees went out of their way to maintain eye contact. They listened better when they looked the speaker straight in the eye. Such an easy thing to do . . . keep eye contact . . . yet it can tremendously improve your listening productivity.

Not only should your eyes keep contact with the speaker, but your ears should as well. A television set turned on in the same room as your conversation . . . other people talking loudly enough for you to hear . . . loud music playing nearby—these and other distracting sounds can draw your mind away from the speaker's message.

Again, take a tip from George Reade: "Focus your ears as well as your eyes on the other fellow . . . tune out all sounds but the speaker's voice." You're at your conversational best when you keep both your eyes and ears in close contact with the speaker.

Controlling your emotions.

It would be very natural to react emotionally if a person said, "There's something you do that's very annoying. I've put up with it as long as I can, and now I've got to tell you about it," or if someone said, "I know you feel strongly about this, but so do I. And I disagree with you. I believe. . . ."

In both cases, the speaker wants to tell you something that's very important to him; and in both cases, an emotional reaction would do you more harm than good. In the first example, it would not help you learn how to get along better with the speaker. In the second, it would not increase your chances of changing the speaker's opinion. That's why you'll notice that good conversationalists always keep their emotions under control . . . they make every effort to listen objectively. They know from experience that they can't respond intelligently to what the other fellow is saying until they know exactly how he feels.

At first blush, learning to control your thoughts, senses and emotions may seem to be time- and effort-consuming, but it isn't really hard . . . all you have to do is keep aware of the need for control. After a short time, it will become second nature for your mind, senses and emotions automatically to clear themselves of distractions as soon as another person starts talking. When this happens, you'll find it easy to concentrate freely on the other fellow, and you'll do a much better job of hearing what he has to say. This surely will increase your reputation as a conversationalist and add more personal enjoyment to your discussions.

HOW TO ANIMATE YOUR LISTENING

If there's one person who can annoy almost anyone, it's the blank-faced listener. Consider this classic example:

> "Johnny, please pick up a loaf of bread on the way home from school," Mary asks her ten-year-old. "Use the change from this dollar to buy a candy bar for yourself while you're at the store." Johnny keeps playing with his plastic soldiers, shooting one down after another in a make-believe war. Mary thrusts the dollar bill under Johnny's nose and asks in a frustrated voice, "Did you hear me?" "Yes, Mom. You want me to get some bread on the way home from school, and you'll let me buy a candy bar with the change."

Surely Johnny is a typical boy, but how often do you run into adults who act the same way? Think about people you know . . . how many let interest show on their face when you talk with them? I'll bet that most of them have deadpan faces. You can stare at them from now to "kingdom come," and you'll never be sure whether they are listening to you . . . thinking their own thoughts . . . or even mentally awake in some cases.

Now think of the most animated person you know . . . recall how she reacts in conversations with you. She makes you feel that she's really interested in you and in what you're saying. Yes sir, she's a real pleasure to talk with!

I keep referring to this highly animated person as a female because women are generally more animated than men. But there's no reason at all why there should be any difference between the sexes on this point. It's easy for anyone to be animated.

Whether you're male or female, try this experiment: first think of something that leaves you feeling unhappy, then make your face look sad. Go ahead . . . force it . . . exaggerate so much that you are sure your face must look totally false. Then look into the mirror. It's strange . . . when you see your expression in the mirror, it isn't as unreal as you had thought it was.

Now look happy. Beam . . . radiate pleasure . . . try so hard that every facial muscle feels strained to the utmost. Take another look in the mirror. Your face isn't really as distorted as you thought; real pleasure shows in your face to a much greater degree than usual. Now that you are getting the hang of it, try a few more expressions. Surprise. Astonishment. Shock. Admiration. Respect. Any other you can think of.

I asked you to try these experiments because when someone talks with you, he can't read your mind . . . the only way he can tell if you're listening is by your outward actions. The best actions you can give are real and revealing facial expressions. Use them. At first you may feel that you're overdoing it . . . that you're twisting your face out of shape; but if you feel this way, just remember how surprised you were when you did the preceding experiments and found that your face wasn't as distorted as you thought. Keep on letting your face reveal your inner feelings, and this listening technique soon will become a natural part of your personality. Once you've mastered the knack of animated listening, you'll be surprised how it'll make you much more welcome in conversational gatherings.

HOW GIVING MAKES YOU
A BETTER LISTENER

It's a "draining" experience to talk to someone who asks you questions and listens to your answers, but adds nothing of his own to the conversation. Although everyone realizes that it's bad manners to monopolize a conversation by constant talking, many don't understand that it's equally bad manners not to talk enough. For example, compare these two typical ice-breaking conversations:

First Conversation

You: "Hi, I'm John Jones."

Tom: "Hi, I'm Tom Smith. Do you live near here?

You: "Yes, I do . . . over on Circle Drive."

Tom: "That's nice. Do you work in the city?"

You: "No. I'm luckier than most; I don't have to commute. I work out here in the suburbs."

Tom: "That's interesting. Is it an easy drive to work or do you run into a lot of traffic?"

Second Conversation

You: "Hi, I'm John Jones."

Tom: "Hi, I'm Tom Smith. I hear that we're neighbors. I live on Friendly Court. Is your home near there?"

You: "Yes, it is . . . right over on Circle Drive."

Tom: "Say, that's close, only a block away. I've noticed that most men living in our neighborhood work in the city like me. Boy, is that commute a grind. Are you one of the weary bunch?"

You: "No, I'm luckier than most and work out here in the suburbs. In fact, my company is only a short twenty minute drive from home."

Tom: "You are lucky! But whenever I go anywhere on weekends, I find the traffic heavy. How's it during the week?"

Which Tom Smith would you enjoy talking with . . . the first draining-dry one . . . or the second give-and-take one? Obviously, the second Tom is a lot more fun. Although he asks as many questions as the first Tom, the basic difference is that the second Tom goes beyond just asking questions . . . he gives out information about himself at the same time his questions are taking information from you.

It's a sad fact of life that many people who act like the first Tom actually believe they are good listeners. They reason that, "I give the other fellow plenty of chance to talk!" It's true they do. Good listening, however, requires more than just giving someone a chance to talk and to express himself. Good listening requires both a giving as well as a taking . . . the people who are conversing should exchange opinions and information. That's why sought-after conversationalists follow these principles:

- Listen and give the other fellow a chance to express himself.
- Add information of your own so the other fellow will feel he's also getting something out of the conversation.

When you play the role of a listener, you should aim for balance between give and take. It's perfectly all right to base your comments on what the other person says, but don't just repeat his thought; rather, add some new facts as Tom did in the second conversation . . . he introduced himself, then added the additional information: "I hear that we're almost neighbors. I live on Friendly Court."

Also, word your comments in a way that shows you understand what the other fellow is saying. Again in the second conversation, when you answered that you worked in the suburbs, Tom remarked, "Whenever I go anywhere on weekends, I find the traffic heavy. How's the driving during the week?"

By giving information while you play a listening role, you'll be helping the other fellow express himself without "draining him dry." That's one sure way to turn any conversation into a rewarding and fulfilling one for everybody involved.

THE SECRET OF HEARING WHAT HE'S REALLY SAYING

Many times the *words* another person says don't convey the real message he wants to communicate. Even though he's not saying what he's thinking, the other fellow still expects you to hear and react to his true thoughts.

Sounds like an impossible situation, but it happens every day. For example, I'm sure you have overheard housewives talking at a party. A conversation could go like this:

> **Betty is telling Sandra how her old dresses don't fit her anymore. "For two weeks now I've been running from store to store trying to find new ones. And what trouble I'm having . . . either the store is out of the smaller sizes or the dresses don't flatter my new figure." When Betty stops for a breath, Sandra immediately picks up the trouble theme and starts telling how she's also running from store to store trying to find clothes that fit. After a few minutes, Betty turns away from Sandra and starts telling Carol about her problems.**

Betty turned away from Sandra because Sandra didn't respond to what Betty was *really* saying: "Am I proud. I lost ten pounds and now my old clothes don't fit anymore." If Sandra had listened carefully to catch Betty's true communication, she wouldn't have annoyed Betty by talking about herself. Rather, she would have won Betty's favor and friendship by congratulating her on her weight loss.

How subtlety often hides meaning. Sandra failed to recognize a very common human trait . . . since many people think it's bad manners to compliment themselves directly, they do it subtly. Similarly, many people don't like to criticize another person to his face. So rather than say what they're really thinking, they make up a white lie. This human trait is so universal that advertising professionals often base ads on it. For example, one TV commercial I've seen centers around Tom, a young man with a personal problem that repels other people:

Scene One

A pretty girl turns Tom down when he asks for a date; but rather than tell him her real reason, she white-lies and says, "Sorry, I'm busy Tuesday night." Tom doesn't listen carefully enough to catch the fact that she isn't saying what's really on her mind . . . she doesn't want to date him because she's turned off by his personal appearance.

Scene Two

A born blabbermouth is talking to Tom at the office water fountain, and accidentally refers to the problem that Tom has.

Last Scene

After using the advertised product to improve his appearance, Tom gets his date with the pretty girl. At dinner she looks at him admiringly; but rather than saying, "You're really nice now that your problem is solved," she says, "You look great. Been on vacation?" Again, the girl uses subtlety . . . she doesn't say what she's thinking.

Although this commercial is obviously exaggerated to make a point, it does illustrate a conversational truth . . . many people don't listen carefully enough to catch whether or not someone is really saying what's on his mind. Good conversationalists have learned two tricks that help them listen between the lines and spot when subtlety is being used. Here's how you can use them too:

You can keep alert. In the example of Sandra and Betty, a good listener easily would have caught the real meaning of what Betty was saying; she wasn't being very subtle. But Sandra didn't hear the true message because she was more interested in talking about herself than in listening to what Betty wanted to say. Therefore, Sandra was not alert . . . she was not being a good listener.

You can look for patterns. Once you're alert and listening attentively, you'll be much more likely to spot those times when someone isn't saying what he's thinking. In the TV commercial, an alert Tom wouldn't have needed a waterfountain blabbermouth to cue him in on his problem. He would have searched for patterns . . . he would have noticed the way people reacted whenever he was near them.

Patterns take many forms. For example, when a specific topic is discussed, someone's ever-so-slight physical pulling away from you is a sure-fire hint that your opinion on that subject disagrees with his. He also can subtly warn you that he disagrees by raising the level of his voice, or by speaking a little faster in a somewhat nervous voice. Tom Renaldi once used this technique with the treasurer of his company. In a conversation, Tom had referred to "loopholes" in the tax law. His treasurer, being sensitive to the political implications of the word "loophole," immediately drew back in his chair. Noting the movement, Tom corrected himself: "I mean tax incentives." The treasurer relaxed and Tom was back in his good graces.

Whatever form the pattern takes, an alert conversationalist finds it easy to listen between the lines . . . to spot the pattern and analyze it . . . then to reply to the real communication. This is the secret that many conversationalists have used to establish their reputations as good listeners. It's such an easy and natural secret to use that there is no reason why you cannot use it too.

PREVENTING THE TRAIT THAT COMPLETELY DESTROYS YOUR EFFECTIVENESS

Of all the personality traits, the one that'll most quickly drive friends away is insincerity. Luckily, nearly everyone is sincere at heart, but even the most sincere person can listen in such a poor way that he gives the appearance of being insincere. Let's look at a few examples.

Untimed Ted

While you're eating lunch together, Ted Smyth expresses interest in your woodworking hobby: "I've often wanted to make an extra dresser for my bedroom, but I'm not sure how to go about it. Could you give me some hints on the best way to make a drawer?"

Naturally you're proud of your woodworking know-how, so you're glad to answer Ted's request for information. You start by explaining the importance of choosing the right wood, then you verbally outline the proper way to join each piece together; and finally you describe how to sand, seal and stain the front piece so that it matches the rest of the wood in the dresser. When you stop, Ted asks, "Why is it so important to choose the right wood?"

What gave Ted the appearance of insincerity was the timing of his question. He should have asked it at the most logical time . . . early in the conversation when you first stressed the importance of choosing the right wood. The poor timing was caused by either slow thinking or a desire not to interrupt. But whatever the cause, Ted damaged his friendship with you by creating the impression of an insincere listener.

Agreeable Charley

For the last two summers your neighbor Charley Kent's lawn has browned out at the first sign of summer heat. Knowing that you once had the same problem, Charley asks you for advice one clear Saturday morning. So you drop what you're doing, go over to his house and dig up a piece of his lawn to show him that it's nothing more than a dried-out mat of dead grass, dead roots and peat moss. You explain, "Grass from new seed will grow in this mat in cool and moist spring weather, but when the summer heat comes, all the new grass dries up and dies. When I had this problem, the county agricultural agent advised me to rotary till."

"That's a lot of work. Isn't there another way?" Charley asks.

"Chemicals will work, but they take years. I'm afraid that rotary tilling is the only solution worth thinking about."

"Guess you're right. OK, I'll rotary till . . . it paid off for you."

You go back home feeling good. Sure, you lost an hour from your busy Saturday morning, but Charley Kent had a real problem and you were able to help him out.

Next Saturday, you see Charley throwing seed right over the old, dried-out mat.

Perhaps Charley's appearance of insincerity came about because he wasn't convinced by what you said. That's fine since he's under no obligation to follow your advice, but he does have a responsibility to be honest and sincere. If Charley disagrees with you, he should say so by thanking you for your advice and admitting that, "You're probably right, but it's too much work and expense to completely replant my lawn." Though you might be disappointed in his decision, you would have to respect him for his honesty and straight-forward sincerity.

Or it may be that he agreed with you at first, then changed

his mind after thinking about the time and expense involved. That's all right too. But he did ask you for advice and you went out of your way to give it. Therefore, he does owe it to you to tell you if he later changes his mind.

In a nutshell, what caused Charley's appearance of insincerity was false agreement . . . he told you one thing and did another.

Dishonest John

When comparing reactions to last Saturday's party with John French, you comment that "Mary was such a gracious hostess." John agrees that he was also "impressed with her personal warmth." When you remark how well the after-dinner games were planned, John agrees that he also "enjoyed the games very much . . . they gave everyone a chance to get to know each other better." You leave the conversation with a good feeling toward John . . . after all, he thinks the same way you do.

Later you meet Sam, another fellow who also had discussed the party with John French. Sam tells how John had said he disliked the party . . . he thought the hostess was a bore and he feels that games are for kids.

John was more than just insincere, he was outright dishonest. All through your conversation he agreed with you. Then he later expressed opposite opinions to someone else. Perhaps he did this because he thinks that the way to make friends is simply to agree with whatever the other fellow says . . . unfortunately for John, dishonest agreement, no matter how well-guided the motive, can only result in friendships lost through insincerity.

On the other hand, if John deliberately lied in order to gain your friendship, then stay clear of him. You don't need this kind of person for a friend.

Inattentive Barbara

Knowing that you invest in the stock market, Barbara Alberts asks how you're doing. When you reply that you just made a 10% profit in one week, her eyes open wide. "My husband's lucky if he makes that much in a year . . . how did you do it?"

"Oh, it's mostly luck and timing," you reply. "And anyhow, investing for quick profit gets quite technical, so I'm sure you'd rather not go into it."

"Oh, please do," she quickly answers. So you explain your system of finding those few stocks which tend to change price quickly; then you study their price patterns carefully. When you think a stock is about to rise in price you quickly buy a few hundred shares, then sell them as soon as they go up two or three points. You keep your explanation as simple as you can and use examples wherever possible. When you are finished, you ask Barbara, "Do you understand?"

"Uh? Oh! Yes, I see. You take a lot of money and invest it for a long time. But you have to be careful to pattern your prices."

Here is insincerity at its pathetic worst. Barbara Alberts is using that oldest of feminine tricks . . . make him like you by encouraging him to talk about one of his interests. There is nothing wrong with this technique, but to use it properly, Barbara must be sincere in her interest and make an honest effort to understand what you say. While Barbara's technique for getting you to talk was good, her inattention caused it to backfire. Instead of liking her because she's interested, you end up resenting her because she's an insincere listener.

Poor timing . . . false agreement . . . outright dishonesty . . . inattentiveness . . . whatever the cause, insincere listening is one bad trait that's guaranteed to destroy the effectiveness of any conversationalist. But there's no reason it should destroy your effectiveness. I'm sure that you're sincere as a person or you wouldn't be reading this book right now. So all you have to do to assure that you never seem to be listening insincerely is simply to conduct yourself in a way that conveys your sincerity to the other person. When you review the examples you just read, you'll find two guidelines running through them:

- First, listen carefully and concentrate on what the other person is saying . . . then you'll automatically ask the right questions at the right time and you'll always be attentive.

- Second, put yourself in the other fellow's shoes and imagine how he'll react to what you say ... then you'll be sure not to be false or dishonest in your conversation because you know this eventually will catch up with you.

These two simple guidelines are both easy to follow and easy to build into your personality. Once they've become a habit you'll be surprised how they'll increase your listening effectiveness ... and how they'll help you win friends among the people you talk with.

3

Automatically Communicating Your Thoughts and Ideas Clearly

Simply by becoming familiar with the easy-to-absorb principles presented in the earlier chapters, you should be instinctively listening much more effectively by now. That's great. So let's flip the coin and look at the other side, for pay-off conversation requires that you both listen and speak well.

When you think about what a conversation is, you'll realize that it's really a form of communicating . . . whenever you speak up, you are transferring a thought from your mind to your listener's mind. The communication can be as simple as conveying a friendly attitude toward a stranger, or it can be as complex as selling a new technical process to a customer's chief engineer.

ELIMINATING THE BIGGEST STUMBLING BLOCK TO UNDERSTANDING

Whether simple or complex, the thought you transfer can't be clearer than the thought you originally formed in your mind. It's the same idea as taking a picture: If you snap the shutter and get a negative that's out of focus, then any picture made from that negative will also be out of focus. Coming back to communication . . . if your thinking is unclear and fuzzy, it's impossible to transmit a clear thought to your listener!

In the following two examples, consider whether you'd rather be Larry or Stan:

Larry's Conversation

Boss: "How's the new Employee Handbook coming along?"

Larry: "It's at the printer's now."

Boss: "Great! Then we'll have it in time for the manager's meeting?"

Larry: "Maybe."

Boss: "Oh? How long does the printing take?"

Larry: "About a week."

Boss: "Good, Since the meeting's a week and a half from now, we should have the handbook by then. Right?"

Larry: "Maybe. Printing takes only a week. But, first we have to make the printing plates . . . and that takes at least three days if everything goes right."

Boss: "Let's see if I understand what you said . . . if everything goes well, the booklet will be finished by the meeting date. Am I right?"

Larry: "You're right."

Boss: (To himself) "Why the devil didn't he say that in the first place? This guy is really a poor communicator."

Stan's Conversation

Boss: "How's the new Employee Handbook coming?"

Stan: "Very good. It's at the printers now. Normally it would be finished in eight working days. So with luck, we'll get it by the manager's meeting. But if anything goes wrong . . ."

Boss: "Fair enough. I'd appreciate it if you'd personally follow the job . . . it would be good to have even a few advance copies for the meeting."

Boss: (To himself) "That's a complete report. He's

a good communicator."

Both Larry and Stan may be equally good in producing printed materials, but the impression they convey to their boss isn't equal. If their boss had to choose between promoting either Larry or Stan, it's a sure bet he'd choose Stan. And the ability to communicate well would be the largest factor in the boss' decision.

The best way to make sure you communicate well is to stop and think before you speak. I remember a former boss of mine who had a sign in his office, "Engage mind before starting tongue." That's an excellent idea, and an easy one to follow . . . just keep quiet until you've first asked yourself, "Do I have a clear mental picture in my mind of what I want to communicate?" If you don't, think for a while until you do have a clear mental picture. Then speak. That's how simple it is to eliminate fuzzy thinking . . . the biggest stumbling block to clear communication, and often the main reason why someone misses out on that big raise or promotion.

HOW SIMPLICITY INCREASES YOUR EFFECTIVENESS

Try to communicate a thought that's too complicated, and you're sure to lose your listener. Yet if you go the other way and oversimplify, you may not get your idea across at all. That's why successful conversationalists walk the middle ground by concentrating on just a few key points.

For example, assume you're looking for a new house, and you've told the real estate agents that you are only interested in three-bedroom houses with a large kitchen and a family room . . . and that the appearance and setting of the house is very important to you. You receive a phone call from an agent trying to convince you to look at a house he has for sale:

Randy Michner's Description

"It is a gold Dutch Colonial with an extension coming off the left side."

Randy put a lot of information in this one sentence . . . he told you the general color, the basic style of architecture, and that the house is longer than deep since an extension comes off the left side. But Randy didn't give you enough information. You can't visualize how the house sets on the land, how large it is, or how many rooms it has. In short, you can't form a good mental picture of the house for sale on the basis of Randy's description. But would you want as detailed a description as Eric's?

Eric Forman's Description

"The house is rectangular and has a black roof that starts down from its peak at a slight slope for about six feet, then continues down at a steep slope, until it reaches the ceiling height of the first floor. No windows from the second floor show through the front of the roof.

"A one-story extension comes off the left side of the house. The first part of the extension sets back about four feet from the main structure and has a roof line running parallel with the main structure's roof. The second part of the extension attaches to the first. Its roof line runs perpendicular to the roof line of the first extension; its front wall is even with the front wall of the main structure.

"Situated on a wooded acre, the house is set at an angle with the left corner of the second extension being closest to the street. In front of the house is a circular bluestone driveway."

If you could make it halfway through Eric's description without getting lost, you're way above average. There's way too much information; it's a rare person who could form a clear mental picture of the house for sale. Finally, consider a third agent's description of the same house. Note how it is much simpler, yet still complete:

Ralph Jenkin's Description

"It's a typical Dutch Colonial with a large black roof, There are no dormers or window wells cut into the front of the roof.

"At one time a breezeway connected the left side of the house to an oversized garage. Both have been converted into living space, with the kitchen extended into the breezeway and the garage turned into a family room.

"The house is set about 60 feet back from the street on a one-acre wooded plot. It has a circular bluestone driveway."

Ralph's description uses just enough detail to give you a fairly accurate mental picture of the house. Note how it uses picture words such as "Dutch Colonial" and "breezeway" to help you clarify your mental image. For example, compare the second paragraph in Eric's description with the second paragraph in Ralph's description. Of these three descriptions, it should be obvious which one has the best chance of convincing you to see the house . . . and thus of earning a healthy commission for the real estate agent.

As these descriptions illustrate, you can use simplicity to clarify your communications by boiling down the details to a few key points, and by using picture words to help your listener visualize the more complex details of the thought you are communicating.

By using simplicity to get across your key points, you'll be sure to keep your listener's attention . . . you'll be a much more effective conversationalist.

HOW TO CONVERSE CLEARLY

I'll bet you've often felt annoyed and said, "This guy is trying to tell me something, but he keeps going in circles. I wish he'd make himself clear." Whenever you think this way, you're on the receiving end of vocal noise; and being only human, you've probably transmitted your share of vocal noise as well.

Vocal noise is words spoken for the speaker's benefit and

not the listener's. The easiest way to recognize vocal noise, and thus to eliminate it from your own conversation, is by working with the following two examples . . . they'll give you an instinctive feel for what vocal noise is and how to avoid it. You can learn a lot just by reading the examples; but to get the most from them, I recommend that you pick up a pencil and paper, then edit each example so that its message is clear and easy to understand. Although there are many ways you could edit these examples, one suggested rewrite of each is given at the end of this chapter for your guidance . . . but you'll discover more if you don't turn to the suggested rewrite until *after* you've finished your own edit. Here are some guidelines to help you:

- Keep in mind the key fact that you communicate only when you successfully transfer a thought from your mind to your listener's mind.
- Before you speak a word, form a clear mental picture of the exact thought you want to convey.
- Communicate only one thought at a time . . . and finish that thought before moving on to the next one.
- Let your thoughts follow each other in a logical order. Your listener should get the meat of your message without any mental gymnastics; he shouldn't have to mentally reorganize what you say.
- Leave out any comment not directly related to the main thought you want to convey.
- Keep objective . . . don't let your own emotions get mixed in with the thought you want to communicate.

With these guidelines in mind, you'll find it an easy job to rewrite the following conversations in a way that helps Rosy and Eddie do a better job of communicating.

Rosy tells a three-in-one.

It's seven o'clock and Rosy and Tony have just finished dinner:

Rosy: "Oh, darling, I've an important question that Al wanted me to ask you. You see, I was shopping at Dresman's today, when guess whom I ran into. Well, it was Mary and Al. Mary had on a purple dress that looked as if it hadn't been to the cleaners in years. Her face was drawn . . . she had bags under her eyes . . . she wasn't wearing make-up at all . . . and Mary usually looks so neat and well-groomed . . . I hope she is OK. Anyway, I ran into them at Dresman's while I was there to buy a new handbag. You know that old bag I use for everyday running around? Well, it is getting so old and worn-looking now . . ."

Tony: "What important question did Al have?"

Rosy: "I'm coming to it . . ."

Tony: "So get there!"

Rosy: "Well! If you're going to be so impatient I'll tell you. He wants you to call him about a golf foursome on Saturday. My, you're impossible to talk to. Most husbands, would never be as rude as you are . . . interrupting all the time . . ."

Eddie tells it to his glory.

The scene is an industrial plant where the manufacturing manager has just asked his general foreman whether a rush job was shipped on time. Eddie answers:

"Did I ship on time? Don't I always get my work done? You should have seen what I went through on that rush job. Without my personal attention it would still be here. First of all, I wasn't told about the job until the last moment . . . this put me behind right from the start. So the only way I could meet the deadline was to follow the job personally, and it's a good thing I did. When I requisitioned the raw material, the stock clerk said it would take two days to deliver the stock to us ... so I went into the warehouse with one of my men and got it myself. Then the lathe broke down. When the maintenance man finally arrived, he didn't know how to fix the machine. So I rolled up my sleeves and showed him how. After we finally got the parts made, I next had to get quality control's OK, but they normally require three days to inspect parts. So to speed them up, I hand-walked the parts through inspection and then personally took them to shipping. Yes sir, I shipped on time. I don't let anything or anyone stop me from doing my job."

As these two examples show, vocal noise is words spoken for the speaker's benefit and not for the listener's ... it's talk that satisfies the speaker's inner needs. It may help a housewife relieve her frustrations after a day spent listening to her young children's unending chatter ... or it may help a "high-ego" employee build up his own sense of importance. There's nothing wrong with conversations that satisfy these inner needs ... because it helps people feel better, vocal noise has a definite place in conversation. But when you want to communicate a thought, vocal noise can only hurt you since it will alienate your listener. When your objective is to convey an idea, communicate it as clearly and concisely as you can. This will win your listener's respect as well as get your idea across.

BEING SURE YOUR LISTENER
HEARS WHAT YOU MEANT TO SAY

The old bromide, "a picture is worth a thousand words," holds true whether you're communicating a thought by speaking it or by writing it. That's because a thought, like a picture, is specific and detailed. And this creates a problem since most of the words you can use to describe the thought are general in meaning.

The problem of using general words. For example, the word "chair" is a general word meaning almost anything you can sit on. Yet when you think about the word, chances are that very specific mental pictures appear in your mind. To illustrate this point, let's assume that your wife asks you to bring another chair into the living roon for Aunt May. The first picture that pops into your mind is a mental image of a kitchen chair . . . it is nearby, lightweight and easy to get and carry back. But when you arrive with the metal chair in hand, your wife explodes: "That eyesore isn't the chair I meant. Bring a nice dining room chair."

At this time, you could either point out that your wife didn't clearly state exactly which chair she wanted or prevent hard feelings by swallowing your frustration and exchanging chairs.

Specific words present problems too. When trying for clear communication, many people try to make their descriptions as photographic as possible by using specific words. But these words create a problem of their own . . . they often require special knowledge on the listener's part before he can fully grasp their meaning. That's when their effectiveness as a conversationalist is hurt. Here's an illustration of what I mean:

Read the following list of words and note which ones create an image of a specific car in your mind:

Chevrolet	Maxwell
Ford	Stanley Steamer
Buick	Cadillac
DeSoto	Bugatti

Obviously, the words that form a mental image are those that name a car you have seen before. The message is clear: Specific words have meaning only when they describe something that your listener has seen or experienced.

I remember vividly one communication gap created by specific words that turned out very fortunately for me. I was a young lad sick in bed, and after a lengthy examination, the doctor told me, "You don't have spinal meningitis, rather you have poliomyelitis. And since the hospitals are all filled, you'll have to fight the disease at home." Week after week passed, but I didn't complain too much . . . to a ten-year-old the chance to stay home from school and receive constant attention was a good deal. What's more, I felt proud when I overheard the doctor telling my parents how courageous I was to "have poliomyelitis and yet to keep such happy spirits."

Only after I was well past the danger point did I ask the doctor, "What is poliomyelitis?" He defined this specific word with two more specific words: "infantile paralysis." I knew what these words meant. He went on to explain, "You have the type of infantile paralysis that attacks the heart and brain, but the crisis is past and you're now out of danger." For the first time I realized how sick I had been . . . and how lucky it was that I didn't understand the specific word "poliomyelitis"! Had I known earlier in my illness what could have happened to me, I probably wouldn't have kept the happy spirits and positive attitude that helped me get well. What the doctor had praised as courage was really a lack of knowledge. The specific word, "poliomyelitis," didn't overlap my experience . . . I didn't have the special knowledge required to understand its meaning.

In this example it was fortunate that the special knowledge was missing. But many times this lack of knowledge leads to misunderstandings and to garbled, unclear communications.

So the key to making sure that your listener hears the same message you send is to realize the limitation of both general and specific words. The easiest way to do this is to let these two guidelines become an everyday part of your conversational personality:

- Define your general words so they mean the same to both you and your listener. (For example, say "dining room chair," rather than just "chair,")
- Only use specific words when you know your listener will understand them. (For example, if you're a dentist talking to a ten-year-old, refer to a cavity's location as being in the "top" of a tooth, not in its "crown.")

In short, there's no deep dark secret to making sure your listener hears the message you send when you talk. All that's required is a little care in choosing the proper words so that the mental image that forms in your listener's mind matches the one you already have in yours. Once both images match, you have communicated . . . you have been an effective conversationalist.

HOW TO CONVERSE WITH MORE
THAN WORDS ALONE

The only time you communicate with words alone is when you're writing a letter. But the moment you can be seen or heard by the other person, your voice inflections and body movements also become part of your communication.

Your voice can say more than your words. For example, suppose you are talking on the phone:

"How are you today?" asks the person at the other end.
"Oh, fine," you answer in a tired, discouraged voice.

Which told the truth: your words or your voice? The way you use your voice is so important that Herbert Hoover once remarked: "Propaganda, even when it sticks to the facts, can be slanted by the magic of the human voice. All of which can be accomplished by emotion and emphasis on words and phrases."

Picture yourself sitting in a large jet plane . . . you're over an airport, surrounded by clouds so dense that you can't see the plane's wing tip. As you prepare to land, you hear one of these announcements come over the public address system:

- You hear these words spoken in a firm and confident voice: "There's a storm going on below with rain and gusty winds, so our landing may be a little bumpy. But there's nothing to worry about; we've landed in much worse weather with no trouble."
- Or you hear these words in a hesitant, unsure voice: "Sorry you can't see the city lights as we land, but there are storm clouds hanging over the area. However, the airport says it's OK to land, so we'll go on in. Please fasten your seat belts."

Which one of these announcements would give you a greater sense of confidence? What would have a greater effect on your thinking . . . the words that you hear or the tone of voice in which they are spoken? These examples clearly show how you can make yourself a better conversationalist simply by using the right tone of voice.

What you see is often as important as what you hear. Suppose you play a practical joke on Tom and later receive a note in the mail that says: "You're a no-good troublemaker. (signed) Tom." Chances are you would think he's mad at you.

But if Tom called you on the phone and said only, "You're a no good troublemaker," then hung up, you would react to more than his words alone. You also would have to consider whether his voice sounded angry or playful.

Finally, if you were to meet Tom on the street and he said in an angry voice, "You're a no good troublemaker," a look at his face would help you understand how he really feels. If you see a twinkle in his eye and a slight smile around the corners of his lips, then you know for sure that he isn't really mad at you over the joke.

Listening with your eyes is a more productive form of communication than many people realize. There are many ways you can use this type of listening to your advantage. For example . . .

- While presenting a new idea to your boss, you note that his hands are relaxed and resting on the arms of his chair. When you finish talking, he seems impressed; he agrees to think about what you said. You're about to leave his office when you wonder if you should try to get him to agree to the new idea right now. Then you look at his hands again . . . they are tightly gripping the chair arms; he is getting impatient, so you leave right away while you're still ahead.

- Later in the day you must correct your assistant for a mistake he's made. You know he's proud and sensitive, and must be handled tactfully. When you call him into your office, he remains standing in a rigid position. This is your first visual communication . . . he's either tense or on the defensive, so you chat casually for a minute until he relaxes. Then you start talking about his mistake, and he shifts his feet restlessly, his muscles tightening. Noting this visual signal, you comment mildly on his error, then discuss the part of the job that he did right. He relaxes. So you return to the error, carefully watching his body movements and keeping ready to add some praise if he reacts too negatively. When the conversation's over, you have explained to your assistant how he can prevent future errors, yet you haven't wrecked his morale or damaged your relationship with him. By using visual communication techniques, you have proven that you know how to use conversation to make you a better supervisor.

You should use more than words alone whenever the other person can hear your voice or see you. With the one exception of a written page, there is no other time when words alone will assure clear communication. The tone of your voice and the movements of both your face and your body play a vital part in clearly communicating your thoughts and ideas . . . and in helping make you a better conversationalist.

One version of an edited Rosy

Rosy's conversation actually consists of three separate thoughts: First, the message that Al wants delivered; second, the fact that Mary looks run down; and third, the fact that Rosy is happy about her new handbag.

When these thoughts are presented separately and in order of importance, Rosy's conversation becomes easily understandable. Here's one way Rosy's thoughts could be edited for clarity:

Rosy: "When I was shopping at Dresman's today, I ran into Al and Mary. Al asked me to pass on a message . . . he's planning a golf foursome for Saturday and would like you to join him. He wants you to call him after supper and let

	him know if you can make it . . ."
Tony:	"Thanks for the message."
Rosy:	"Oh, you're welcome. I thought you'd want to go, but I didn't want to say 'yes' for you. So I told him you'd call. One thing bothered me though . . . Mary didn't look well at all. You know how she's always so careful about how she looks? Well, her dress was wrinkled and dirty . . . it needed cleaning badly. And her face looked drawn . . . she had bags under her eyes . . . and she wasn't wearing make-up. I'm worried about her . . ."
Tony:	"Let me see if I can find out how she's feeling on Saturday when I see Al."
Rosy:	"Oh, that's a good idea. I don't want to stick my nose into her business, but if she needs help I don't want to sit by. I'll wait until you talk to Al before I do anything. By the way, while I was at Dresman's, I bought a new handbag. You know the old one I have for everyday use . . ."
Tony:	"It's getting pretty worn."
Rosy:	"Yes, you're right . . . it looks very threadbare. That's why I couldn't resist buying a very practical black bag that Dresman's had on sale. Let me get it and show it to you . . ."

One version of an edited Eddie

Very obviously, Eddie was letting his ego dominate his conversation. All his boss wanted was a simple yes or no. And Eddie could have told him this, plus communicating how hard he had worked, by first answering his boss and then suggesting a better way to handle similiar problems in the future. This approach would make him look good to his boss by proving how hard he worked on this job, and by showing that he was alert enough to spot ways to prevent future emergencies from taking so much time. Such a conversation could go as follows:

"Yes, sir, the rush job was shipped on time. But I wonder if we made a profit on that order when you consider all the special handling it took. I think I've found a way to hold down costs on future rushes. We could set up a red tag system.

"A normal job is scheduled far enough ahead that the stock clerk has two days to deliver material . . . quality control is given three days to inspect . . . and two days are added as a safety factor in case of machine breakdowns. Now, the only way to speed up a job is to hand-walk it through each step as I had to do on this past one.

"Why not have each rush job given a red tag? Then whenever any department sees that tag, they'll give the job top priority and handle it immediately, putting it ahead of other jobs. This way we'll get on-time delivery without the high costs of special supervision."

4

Short Cuts for Instantly Deciding How to Converse With Any Stranger

Life moves so fast today that you're almost certain to meet someone new at least twice every week. And the time-proven techniques that you've absorbed from the earlier chapters of this book will help you to have pleasant conversations with these strangers. But you want more than just pleasant discussions . . . you want productive, pay-off conversations. And when you're with a stranger, this means you instantly want to decide how to talk with him. Let's look at two basic appeals that work with any stranger, then let's discuss seven short cuts that help you quickly choose the best approach for starting a pay-off conversation with him.

How to appeal to his interests. Perhaps the person who's most vitally concerned with appealing to a stranger's interests is the salesman:

- If you were a shoe salesman you couldn't interest a "prospect" in buying until you first knew if he were looking for a dress shoe, a casual loafer or a hiking boot.
- If you were a new car salesman you couldn't start your sales pitch until you first asked your "prospect" if he wanted a sedan, a station wagon or a sports model.

While you might not have to "sell" anyone in your conversations, you do face a similar situation . . . you must capture your conversation partner's attention by discovering which topics interest him and which ones don't.

And the easiest way to find these interests is to act as a salesman and ask questions. Professional conversationalists, like salesmen, don't waste time guessing, and you shouldn't either. It's so much easier to let the other fellow tell you what his interests are. Then all you have to do to start a lively conversation is to get him talking about these interests.

For example, when Lyle Rosen wanted to get to know a new neighbor, he opened the conversation by welcoming him to the neighborhood. Then, knowing that all men like to talk about their work, Lyle asked, "I notice you have two cars. Have to drive far to work?" This started things off nicely; before long the new neighbor was talking about his job . . . and Lyle was learning many facts he could use to spark future conversations with his new acquaintance.

How to appeal to his emotions. All of us have emotions; they're a strong and permanent part of our personality. In fact, they're so strong, we often find ourselves thinking emotionally no matter how hard we try to remain objective and clear-headed. That's why appealing to a stranger's emotions is one of your best conversation-starting tools . . . especially when you appeal to someone's emotions at the same time you're talking about his interests—for then you give him a feeling of fullness . . . you completely involve him in the conversation.

The easiest way to decide which emotions you should appeal to is by using your intuition as Lyle Rosen did when talking with his new neighbor. Lyle not only drew on the obvious fact that men are interested in talking about their work, but he also carefully observed his neighbor as he talked. Try this technique yourself . . . keep your eyes, ears and other senses wide open when talking with someone else. You'll be surprised at the insights you'll get into his feelings . . . into his likes and dislikes. When his emotions are positive, for example, his eyes will appear a little brighter and more excited than usual, or his voice will sound a little more enthusiastic. You can spot negative emotions by noting a discouraged tone in his voice or a slight pulling away or tensing of his muscles when he talks about certain subjects. By observing someone's reactions for a while, you'll soon find yourself developing a natural insight into his emotional makeup. You'll also be able to guess fairly well how strong a grip these emotions hold on his thinking.

You'll be at your best when you focus your full attention on the reactions, feelings and words of the other person and not on your own thoughts. Don't worry about what you'll say; think only about what he is communicating . . . both with the words he is speaking and with the emotions he is expressing. Do this and when it's your turn to speak, you'll automatically know how to appeal to his emotions.

Using short cuts to draw total strangers into conversation.
When you're face-to-face with a stranger and you want to start a conversation with him, you'll want a quick way to get some clues about his interests and emotions. Given below are seven general groupings of personality types that will help you quickly size up a stranger. Try these short cuts for a while and you'll be surprised how fast you'll become adept at using them. Before you know it, you'll not only be enjoying rewarding conversations with strangers, but you'll also find yourself developing natural starting points that will help you get to know the new person better.

SHORT CUT 1
DECIDING HOW DYNAMIC HE IS

Assume that you have just introduced yourself to a stranger, made a few friendly comments, and then stopped talking to give him a chance to speak. And his reaction is . . . silence. It's an awkward situation, you're up against a quiet person who has thrown the conversational ball right back into your lap; and unless you take the lead a conversation won't start up. But don't let his silence bother you . . . rather take the initiative by using the same short cut that my conversationalist friend, George Reade, uses . . . ask yourself questions until you discover why the stranger is quiet.

. . . Is he quiet because this is the way he wants to be?
Many quiet people I know have all the knowledge and ability they need to hold excellent conversations, but they are reserved and prefer not to speak out until they have a good reason to do so. There is a simple way to tell if the other fellow is this type

of quiet person . . . just search for his interests:

> "I notice you're wearing a Kiwanis emblem. I'm a
> Kiwanian also. In which town are you a member?"
> "Judging by your tan, you must spend a lot of time
> outdoors. Could you be a weekend fisherman like
> myself?"

If your questions start him talking, then you've broken through his reserve and started a discussion. But if your first three or four questions receive short and uninterested answers, then back away. Odds are that this fellow wants to be alone and isn't interested in conversing at the present time.

. . . *Is he a specialized perfectionist?* This type of quiet person has very strong opinions on how other people should act, and which topics are safe to discuss and which ones aren't. He's usually so set in his ideas that he'll look down on anyone who doesn't act and talk exactly as he does. Further, the specialized perfectionist rarely takes the lead in a conversation; he prefers to stay in the background and "let you make the mistakes."

Most people feel uncomfortable when talking with this kind of person and therefore try to keep away from him. But sometimes this isn't possible; you're thrown together with this type in a situation where you must talk with him. What I usually do in a case like this is go slow . . . I gradually speak up in much the same way as I would slowly enter the water at a strange beach . . . one slow step after another . . . carefully searching for hidden holes or toe-stubbing rocks.

. . . *Or is he simply waiting for a spark to set him afire?* There are many people who are more than willing to join in a lively conversation, but they are quiet by nature and need someone to help them get started. So when you're with this type of person, go ahead and take the conversational lead. And do so with enthusiasm. This down-to-earth quiet person is more than willing to join in the fun: all he needs is someone to set the pace. So take the lead and you'll soon find yourself in the middle of a fun-filled conversation.

So far we've been discussing what you would do when you

meet a quiet person. Now let's turn the coin over and see the other side by discussing how to handle yourself when exposed to a dynamic person. In the same way as you did with the quiet person, you find the answer by asking yourself questions:

. . . *Is he just a naturally forceful person?* If he is, and you also have a natural enthusiasm, then by all means don't hold back . . . let yourself go and the two of you will enjoy an animated conversation.

. . . *Is he dynamic because of a recent experience?* For example, I can remember meeting Larry Beam just after he had been highly praised by his boss for doing an outstanding job. Though Larry didn't talk directly about the praise he received, his ego was definitely riding high . . . he wanted center stage in the conversation. I instinctively knew that if I "came on strong," I'd only annoy him. So I gave him my full attention and let him do most of the talking. As as a result, I know Larry took a liking to me.

If you suspect that someone's recent ego-raising is the cause of his dynamic conversation, then follow the same principle I did . . . don't compete with him, he'll only resent you if you do anything to interrupt his moment of glory. The best thing you can do is sit back and be a good listener.

. . . *Or is he hiding a feeling of inferiority behind a dynamic appearance?* There's no good reason in this wide world for anyone to feel inferior . . . sure, everyone has weak points as well as strong ones, but this doesn't mean he's no good. Yet some people think only about their weaknesses; they build them up so much in their minds that their thinking goes haywire . . . they actually come to believe they're not as good as others. One way many people cover up this inferiority feeling is by talking in a dominating and dynamic way. If you get a "gut feeling" that an inferiority complex is the cause of a stranger's talk, again be a good listener and let him take the conversational lead. He'll appreciate your understanding and think well of you for it.

SHORT CUT 2
JUDGING HIS INTELLECTUAL LEVEL

As in Short Cut 1, the simple technique you use in judging

his intelligence level is to ask yourself questions. In fact, you don't even have to ask these questions consciously . . . simply by being aware that you want to know his intelligence level, your mind will unconsciously feed you the information you need. Here's what to look for:

What to do if he talks like a walking dictionary. People who have far-above-average intelligence usually read highly scientific or philosophic journals, and they prefer to converse with other intellectuals. Result: they have problems bringing their vocabulary "down to earth" where they can talk easily with the average Joe. The best way to handle this fellow is to be yourself. If you're also an intellectual, converse on the same vocabulary level as the other fellow. Or if you're an average guy like me, then listen carefully; there's much you can learn. If you're having trouble understanding what he's saying, then do what I do . . . admit you are puzzled, and ask questions until he re-explains his ideas in a way you can understand.

By relaxing and being yourself, you can win his respect. He's smart enough to see through any attempt you make to pass yourself off as one of the "brainy types." So converse in everyday language, speak out only on subjects where you have knowledge, and he'll respect you for what you are. In fact, I've found that he'll often steer the conversation into subjects where I have strong knowledge and thereby create an enjoyable, interesting conversation.

How to react when someone puts on an act. Not everyone who sounds like an intellectual really is one. You'll sometimes meet a fellow who puts on an act . . . either because he feels insecure or because he wants to impress you. The easiest way to spot this type is to listen carefully during the first few moments of conversation. If he comes on too strong or uses ten-dollar words and fancy expressions where there's no need to do so, you can be pretty sure you're talking to an actor.

Again, react by being yourself. Realize that he probably feels insecure, so put him at ease by keeping relaxed and natural. Converse in simple language. Listen attentively. Express interest in what he says. Show respect for him as a person. Soon he'll catch the between-the-lines message of your conversation . . . "There's no need to put on an act with me. I like you and accept you as you are." Chances are he'll then relax and talk naturally; you'll have created another enjoyable conversation.

Handling an average down-to-earth guy. Most people you meet are intelligent, feet-on-the-ground types who don't try to put on any airs. With this kind of person you don't have to do anything special . . . just relax and converse as you normally do. Soon you'll be well on your way toward another rewarding, pay-off conversation.

SHORT CUT 3
GUESSING HOW STRONG-WILLED HE IS

Stubborn as a mule! Wishy-washy! Thick skulled! Thin skinned! Expressions like these have worked their way into our language because they're descriptive . . . you meet people like them all the time. And after a few moments of conversation with a stranger, you usually can tell instinctively if he fits any of these descriptions. This helps you decide whether to take an aggressive or a quiet approach when talking with him.

What type of approach you take depends on what you want to achieve in the conversation. For example, let's assume that you've come up with a new idea and you want to convince other people that it's a good one. In this example, the other fellow's personality is the key to the style you'll use.

How to convince someone who's basically aggressive. Since this person likes to dominate a conversation and feel that he's in control, you don't want to compete with him by pushing your idea too hard. What conversationalist George Reade does when he wants to convince an aggressive person is to tell him about the idea, then start finding things wrong with it. Being aggressive, the other person usually reacts by defending George's idea, by trying to convince him that the idea is a good one. Using this simple technique, George has sold many an idea . . . what actually happens is that the other fellow ends up convincing himself about the advantages of George's idea.

How to convince a quiet and sensitive person. Being aggressive would probably scare a sensitive person away, so start off the same way as George did in the previous example . . . mention the idea to him. But instead of finding things wrong about the idea, act unsure about it . . . ask him for advice, encourage him to offer his opinion. Chances are he'll carefully consider the idea before answering. And, if your idea is a good one, he'll end up "selling" himself on the idea as he considers it.

How to talk to people who have a hard time reaching a decision. So far, we've discussed how you can get a fellow to convince himself that your idea is a good one. The approaches we've looked at don't work on someone who can't make decisions easily. This type needs to be led more strongly . . . he wants to be told what's best for him. This requires a four-step process:

- First, tell him why your idea is a good one.
- Second, show him how he can benefit from it.
- Third, automatically assume that he goes along with your idea.
- Fourth, assure him that he has made the right decision.

For example, when salesman Tom Smathers wanted to sell income protection insurance to an indecisive John Railes, Tom asked him what he would do if he suddenly became sick and his income stopped. As John thought about the question, he realized that income protection insurance might be a good idea. Then Tom showed him a chart listing his expenses on one side, and income from the insurance plan on the other side . . . in other words Tom demonstrated how John could benefit from the idea. Next, Tom automatically assumed that John agreed with him since he didn't offer any objections. To finalize the sale Tom told John about many people who had become disabled, but who were able to keep their family's head above water because of the insurance income . . . he kept assuring him that buying this insurance was the best thing he could do to protect his family. Result: Tom made a sale and earned a commission, and indecisive John felt more secure because he knew he was doing a wise job of providing for his family.

Naturally, when using this approach you have to be somewhat aggressive. And the way in which you assert yourself will depend on the other fellow's personality. If he's sensitive, then be quietly aggressive. If he's strong willed, handle him in the way described next.

And how to talk to a strong-willed individualist. This guy strongly believes in himself and has complete confidence in his ability to make a correct decision on the merits of your idea. He'll be willing to listen to what you have to say, but he'll insist on making his own decision. So the best way to convince him that your idea is good is to describe it in the most factual and dramatic way that you can. This will put the odds in your favor when he decides whether or not he likes your idea.

SHORT CUT 4
EVALUATING HOW REALISTIC HE IS

After you've been talking with someone for a few minutes you'll be surprised at how fast you're gaining insight into the way he approaches life . . . whether he's an idealist and somewhat of a dreamer . . . or whether he's realistic and practical.

Here's the best way to socially converse with an idealist. You know how this person thinks . . . he lets his ideals cloud his mind and thus loses his ability to see life and to talk about it as it really is. Therefore, talk casually with him and stay away from any of the harder facts of life. Stick to discussing only pleasant subjects or else he'll probably get so upset that you won't be able to continue conversing with him.

To get an idealist to accept an unpleasant fact of life, do as Roger Stick does. Roger's job is supervising a large group of office workers, many of them young. And quite a few of these younger workers grew up with easy-going parents. They pretty much did what they wanted; their parents set few, if any, rules. Thus it's hard for them to accept that they now must follow company rules and regulations in order to hold onto their jobs. For example, many of the brighter ones believe that their time is productively spent only when they're producing work. So you can imagine the answer Roger gets when he asks one of these bright youngsters, "John, have you put together the progress report yet on the Reynald's project?" Chances are this question will evoke the answer, "Haven't got time to waste writing reports about what I've done. I know my job. Leave me alone; let me work and the Reynald's project will be out on time."

Although John's dedication to his work and his belief in himself are admirable, his attitude is not realistic. Roger is forced to answer, "Let's be practical. Management asks for these reports because they need them in order to co-ordinate all the projects properly." And if John continues to protest, Roger must flatly state, "Management needs to know what's going on, and it's their right to ask for reports. You'll just have to accept that fact, John. Writing reports is a required part of your job."

Yes, talking tough is often the only way to make an idealist accept unpleasant facts. And when Roger talks this way, he is prepared to fire the employee if he does not respond properly. This might sound like a heartless approach, but as Roger says, "If I don't talk this way I'll be fired for not doing my job. Straight from the shoulder talk can often do a lot of good in helping idealists adjust to the world they work in!"

A conversational technique for handling realists. You can't converse with every realist in the exact same manner, they don't all respond to the same approach. Each one's viewpoint will vary, depending on his past experiences. Many will have strong opinions, and they'll hold to them stubbornly ... thus forcing you to be non-controversial in what you say if you want to avoid an argument. Others will be more open-minded and objective; you can converse more freely with them.

But there's one thing you can be sure of ... they'll all have practical approaches to life. So the one common technique you can use is to keep your verbal feet on the ground and talk realistically ... stay away from the theoretical and the idealistic when you're conversing with a realist.

SHORT CUT 5
DEALING WITH HIS EGO

Whenever you talk to someone for a while, it's only a matter of time before you bump up against his ego ... everyone is self-centered to some degree.

How to react when you're with a "low-ego" person. There's no need to converse in any special way ... just give him normal courtesy and attention. Showing sincere interest in him as a person and honest respect for his ideas will quickly put you into his good graces.

How to handle someone with a highly developed ego. The short cut you use with a high-ego person depends on what you want to accomplish. If you simply want to win his good will, then listen more than you talk, speak only about topics that interest him, and be sure to compliment him sincerely at least two or three times in the conversation.

The real challenge comes when your relationship with a high-ego person goes beyond the talking-to-a-stranger stage. For example, supervising him on the job takes a special technique . . . he usually doesn't like to be told what to do. If you use the short cut described for handling someone like this, you'll do a great deal of listening. Yet obviously you can't afford to spend your whole day listening or you'd never get your own work done. A highly respected and successful business manager, Robert Trench, once explained to me his simple technique for handling high-ego employees: "I talk with the fellow for a while and get him to set a goal for himself. Then I show him how he can satisfy his ego needs by achieving this goal. Once he's taken on this goal as his own, he'll push ahead and I can go on to other work."

SHORT CUT 6
OVERCOMING CHRONIC NEGATIVISM

A "professional negative" is a special type of person. I'm sure you know quite a few; they're all around you. Ask Sally, "How are you?" And she'll answer, "Oh, all right, I guess. But . . ." Then she'll let loose with a list of ailments long enough to keep a hospital staff busy full-time.

Jack is the original feel-sorry-for-me-because-everything-goes-wrong kid . . . in ten minutes he can convince you that he and Lady Luck aren't even on nodding terms.

Sam is constantly at war with "them," and he's always losing. "They" conspired against him by raising his school taxes . . . "they" wouldn't allow some deductions he took on his income tax . . . "they" overcharged him when his car was repaired. Poor Sam should have been born a hermit in the middle of a jungle.

Your conversations will be much more fun if you can keep away from professional negatives like these, but unfortunately you can't always do this . . . you often have to talk with them on the job or at social affairs. Then the easiest thing for you to do is to steer the conversation away from personal problems. This will improve your chances of having a pleasant discussion.

SHORT CUT 7
DETERMINING HOW OPEN-MINDED HE IS

As you know from your personal experience, some people you meet will be objective and open-minded in their thinking; others will be emotional and closed-minded.

How you can spot closed-minded people. One common trait these people have is forming their opinions on a whim and rarely looking into the facts . . . when election time comes, for example, they'll vote for the political candidate whose personality appeals to them, rather than voting for the candidate who's best qualified. Yet once these emotion-dominated people form an opinion, they hold to it with an almost do-or-die attitude . . . they close their mind to all ideas that differ from their own.

Another trait to look for: many of them think in a very petty way. Tim, for example, is rarely concerned about anything not directly related to his own daily life. And even within this narrow area, he doesn't want to think very much . . . he prefers to notice just surface appearances. A typical Tim reaction: If a fellow worker sent him a memo outlining a new idea that would help him do a better job, he'd probably comment to others about how badly the memo was worded rather than consider the merits or demerits of the idea itself. In short, he rarely digs beneath the surface since that would take more mental energy than he cares to exert.

When conversing with people like Tim, you can shift into neutral and coast along . . . you won't have to stretch your mind. But keep your guard up, say only safe things, and be careful not to disagree with his opinions. Otherwise you'll be the target for his comments when you're not around.

Of course, if you don't care what this type of person says about you, then let yourself go ... who knows, maybe you can add some excitement to his dull and unchanging world.

Consider whether it's worth your time to open up a closed mind. I'm sure you've had the same experience I've had with this type ... the more you suggest that he change his opinions, the harder he will cling to them. He formed them emotionally; he'll defend them emotionally.

Yes, you can get him to change his mind ... but it'll take a lot of conversation. First, you'll have to talk with him until you uncover the emotional attitude around which he formed his opinion. Then you'll slowly have to cause him to change his attitude. Chances are he'll then change his opinion too. But this is a long, time-consuming job and usually isn't worth all the effort unless you have an important reason for wanting him to change. In casual and first-time conversations it's much easier and simpler just to change the subject.

What the open-minded person is like. He'll also notice what is going on around him, but he's interested not only in what happens, but why it happens as well. For example:

When watching the hometown football team play their Saturday game, Charley Alberts looks at more than just the scoreboard ... he also notes the strengths of the hometown team and the weaknesses of the visiting team. Then later Charley is able to discuss any fine points of the game, from the accurate passing of a quarterback to the linebacker action on the defensive team. And Charley's interests range across many areas. For example, on the subject of China, Charley can discuss at length such subjects as Mao's guerrilla and military tactics as used by Asian Communists, and the historical background of China and how she has been continually dominated by dynasties, foreigners and war lords.

How you can influence the opinions of an open-minded person. This person is objective ... he'll form strong opinions; but unlike the emotional, closed-minded person, he's more than willing to change his opinion if you can give him information that proves your point of view is right.

So if you want to influence an open-minded person, present as many facts as you can think of that bear on the point you wish to make. Being objective, the other person will surely weigh these facts carefully and change his opinion if he is wrong. This is the short cut that the sought-after conversationalist George Reade uses very successfully when he finds himself at odds with an objective person whom he has just met.

When reading these short cuts, you probably noticed that each one presents the extremes of personality found within each classification. Obviously, most people fall in between these extremes; but just the same, these short-cut groupings will help you quickly guess a stranger's personality, and thus they'll help you through the first few minutes of conversation with someone new.

They also can help you get to know the new fellow's personality faster. As his strangeness and newness fade away, you'll find that the short cuts will help pinpoint your new acquaintance's interests and emotions. Once this is done you'll be well on your way toward making a new friend and enjoying a pay-off conversation.

5

Developing the Timing Instincts That Make You an Outstanding Conversationalist

Knowing exactly when is the right moment to speak up or keep quiet is a very profitable asset. Good timing is a vital part of your life . . . ask the boss for a go-ahead on a pet project and you have the best chance for a "yes" answer if you hit him when his mood is right . . . steer away from a critical remark when your wife is tired and you'll preserve domestic harmony. Whether in business, at home or in social situations, knowing when to speak, listen or change the subject can make you a more popular and successful conversationalist. And it isn't hard to develop the good timing instincts that lead to pay-off conversations . . . you can learn them quickly and simply by becoming familiar with the following conversational techniques.

HOW TO SHARPEN YOUR SENSE OF TIMING

The easiest way to increase your popularity through sharper conversational timing is to put yourself in the other fellow's shoes. Ask yourself: "How is he feeling? Is he enthusiastic or tired? Ready to listen or preoccupied? Discouraged or optimistic?" And so on. You don't have to make a big chore out of it and psychoanalyze his personality . . . you just have to decide what kind of mood he's in at the moment. Then you can talk with him in the way that best matches how he feels. This assures that he will be receptive to you and enjoy conversing with you.

Reacting to the other fellow's excitement . . .

At one time or another, everyone becomes enthusiastic

about an idea he has. You've seen it happen . . . a friend becomes so excited about his idea, so eager to tell you about it, that he is literally bursting with talk.

Suppose, for example, you phone Diana Long and ask her to serve on a Special Projects committee for your club. After the opening greetings, Diana starts talking excitedly:

Diana: "Did you hear about the Halloween party I'm helping our church plan for the youngsters?"

You: "A party's a good idea . . . it'll keep the kids off the street and out of trouble. Are you going to do anything special to amuse the kids?"

Diana: "Well, we'll have refreshments, of course . . . and, guess what? Some of the teenagers volunteered to help out with a special chamber of spooks. When a younger child arrives, we'll send him down a dark hallway where wet threads hanging from the ceiling will brush against his face. Just beyond that a teenager will blink a flashlight, first at the child to startle him, then at a skeleton. While doing this he will say . . ."

On races Diana's voice as she describes every detail of the party. Finally she finishes off by saying, "Well I have to run now. I'll call you later and let you know how the party turns out."

Let's assume that halfway through her description Diana's voice stops for a few seconds. Instinct alone would tell you this isn't a good time to ask her to join the Special Projects Committee. The timing is wrong; Diana hasn't stopped talking . . . she's merely pausing for breath . . . or to gather her thoughts . . . or to seek the right word. While her vocal cords aren't busy her mind is; she's talking just as much as if she were moving her lips. And, as you know from experience, when a person is bursting with talk, he's not ready to listen. His mind isn't ready to pay attention to what you have to say.

The easiest way to handle the situation and to win her gratitude at the same time is to be a good listener. Comment on her ideas in a way that shows you're impressed with how she's planning the party: "A chamber of spooks will go over big with the kids. And the wet strings . . . how creative!"

Common sense tells you not to change the topic in situations like this; the other person just isn't ready to listen. But you can mention at the end of the conversation that "I'd like to talk with you about a new committee our club is forming. I'll call you later in the week to discuss it." When someone is bursting with talk, react by listening well . . . your reputation as a conversationalist will surely grow . . . and the odds will be much greater that the other person will respond positively to any request you have at a later time.

What to do when you're enthusiastic, but the other fellow is tired or wrapped up in his own thoughts . . .

Assume you're managing a department so overloaded with work that your employees are about ready to quit in frustration. To complicate things, the company has a hiring freeze on so you can't hire anyone new. For some weeks now you've been seeking a solution that'll get you out of the bind you're in. Finally an idea pops into your mind: "The Sales Order department isn't as busy as usual. I'll borrow one of their people for a week or two." So you head for your boss' office to get his approval. When you get there, you put yourself in his shoes . . . you notice that his face looks tired and that he seems preoccupied with problems of his own. You decide not to launch right into a sales pitch on your idea; you realize that you'd better first test to see if the timing is right . . . switching people from one department to another can be complex; it will take much of your boss' time and energy to settle all the details.

So you use an old conversational trick . . . you bring along a solution to a simple problem, as well as the facts of the more complex one. Then you test the boss' mood by discussing the easier problem first. If he is impatient and seems eager to get back to his own problems, you don't bring up the subject of switching people at that time. You know your boss is too wrapped up in his own problems at the moment to give your idea much of a hearing . . . in fact, his first thought will probably be, "Say anything that'll end this interruption." And that "anything" almost certainly will be an outright "no." Simply by waiting a day or two before bringing up your problem, you'll increase your chances of success tenfold.

The moral of this example: when the other fellow is tired or wrapped up in his own thoughts, reject your own desire for quick and immediate action . . . let his feelings determine your timing. You can always talk to him later when he is less preoccupied and in a better mood to listen to your idea . . . your chances of getting a "yes" answer will be much better then.

What to do when the other fellow's ego is riding high . . .

Jerry Richter has just returned from Salt Lake City where he sold a big order to a difficult customer. At the lunch table, Jerry dominates the conversation as he paints a fascinating word-picture of the city and its Mormon founders . . . everyone's interest is tightly held by his skill as a weaver of words.

When he ends his story, you could speak up and tell some of the things you know about Salt Lake City. But again, your common sense says no . . . the timing is wrong. The way he told his story shows that Jerry is still selling; he's still using words to shape the thoughts of others. At this time Jerry isn't the least bit interested in what anyone else has to say . . . his ego is riding high and he wants to give it an outlet by talking. So don't compete with him by speaking up. Win his friendship the simple way . . . by being a good listener. Any other action will only antagonize him.

What to do when the other fellow wants to unwind a bit . . .

You and some co-workers are taking a mid-morning break in the cafeteria. The coffee cups are half drained; conversation is of the light and kidding type with Jerry Richter again taking the lead. The easy atmosphere exists of a relaxed group at home with each other. Common sense again says this isn't the time to bring up a business problem you wanted to discuss with Jerry. The kidding nature of his talk is a warning that Jerry wants to relax this time. In fact, his conversation is mechanical and unoriginal. Obviously, he isn't in the mood to talk business. So let him unwind and relax over coffee. Then, when he is back at his desk, approach him with your business problem . . . your chances of getting his cooperation will be much better then.

As these examples show, the easiest way to increase your popularity and to finely hone your sense of conversational timing is always to put yourself in the other fellow's shoes. And this means putting his personal feelings ahead of your own.

KEEPING YOUR LISTENERS ATTENTIVE

Now that you're becoming more adept at conversational timing, let's see how you can put this timing to work making others more attentive when they talk with you. As you know from previous conversations, the other fellow will always pay more attention when you're talking about a topic he knows something about. People are just naturally more interested in discussions that tie into their own interests, their educational level or their personal experience.

How to aim your conversation at their interests . . .

One weekend, a conversationalist friend of mine, Larry Johnson, went to the theater and saw a well-acted play that had some great comic stories in it. On Monday he was still enthusiastic about the play and anxious to share some of the jokes with his co-workers, so in the morning he wandered out to the cafeteria for a coffee break and sat down with some fellows that he knew enjoyed a good laugh. But before Larry said anything, he first put himself into his co-worker's shoes by listening to their remarks; he wanted to catch what direction the conversation was taking before he shared his new jokes. It was September . . . the pennant race was hot and so was the conversation:

> "The Dodgers have got it easy."
> "Are you kidding—look at the teams they still have to play. It's anyone's pennant."
> "Yeh, name another team as good as theirs."
> "That's what you say. Look at the record."

It's a good thing Larry listened before he spoke; joke lines from a play is nowhere near this group's current interest. At lunchtime, however, he was eating with a different group. Eric remarks, "Did you see that TV show last night where Alan Sparks had to act the part of a woman?"

Now the timing was right . . . they were talking about a topic related to the one Larry wanted to discuss.

The listening-before-you-speak process is too vital to bypass. Everyone has many interests that change from time to time. So use the same technique that has made Larry such a well-liked conversationalist . . . before you speak up in any conversation, first open your ears to learn what the group is talking about. Then speak up on the topic that is holding their interests at the moment.

How to key your conversation into their educational level . . .

Assume that after a PTA meeting you get into a discussion about the high cost of living with some of the other parents. They're all complaining about rising costs . . . the women are especially upset about the "impossible" prices of food and clothing.

This is a topic you've read up on. For instance, you know that beef will soon be in short supply since ranchers are holding cattle back from market to use them as breeding stock. Pork is also in short supply; however, there are plenty of chickens around and their supply is currently increasing. Thus, in the next few months beef and pork prices will climb even higher but chicken prices should hold even.

Yes, you are loaded with information and can speak with authority; you really can add facts to the conversation. But again, before talking put yourself in the other fellow's shoes by looking around and noting who is present.

Sam and Joan are there; they are pleasant people, but not very well-informed. And, the narrow viewpoints on life held by Jack and Mary don't imply a very broad outlook either.

So hold back your comments until you are with a better informed group . . . these people won't think much of you if you talk over their heads. This isn't the best time to go deeply into agricultural economics; the timing's better for general complaints about high prices . . . and the devil with the reasons why.

The next Friday night you are at a church affair talking with Charley Jones and Jerry Lent; the topic again is the soaring cost of living. "Aha,"you think, "Charley and Jerry both teach at the local college . . . now is the time to speak up and unload some of my knowledge." For openers you drop some well-thought-through remarks on the economic picture. Charley and Jerry react quickly to your cue and the discussion is on; now is your chance to shine.

But wait. What is Charley saying? Statistics on Gross National Product . . . last year actual, this year anticipated, next year forecasted. Jerry is talking about Keynesian economics and how this theory relates to today's problems. Perhaps this is the time to play the good listener role, these two fellows are far ahead of you when it comes to knowing the facts.

Yes, keeping your listeners attentive requires more than just knowing a lot of facts . . . it means evaluating the knowledge you have and keying it into the educational level of the others present. This way you can talk in a way that'll make you sound like one of them. They'll respect you for this.

How to tie your conversation into their personal experience. Haven't you often suffered through conversations where people discuss topics that don't touch on your experience:

- You're at a party when the Smiths and the Murphys discover that they all grew up in the same home town. Within minutes they're talking about mutual friends, local events and other topics where they share a common experience.
- At another party, you're talking to Andy and Phil when a chance remark uncovers that they had both worked for Union Paper earlier in their careers. Again an "old-times" discussion springs up.

Conversations like these are so boring that it's hard to stifle a yawn. So you need to do something positive. For example, you could start a side conversation with some of the others present, or sit politely and listen, or make yourself useful to the host or hostess. None of these actions will offend the people who are conversing.

In the preceding examples, the other people didn't tie their conversation into your experience. And you reacted quite naturally by losing interest. It's natural that other people will react in the same way if you start discussing a topic that doesn't tie into their experience. Therefore, when introducing a new topic, first stop and consider the background of the others present. If the topic you've chosen matches their experience, launch the discussion ... the timing is right. But if the topic doesn't tie into their experience, then use these easy-to-follow guidelines:

- If the other people enjoy discussing new topics, go ahead. But carefully watch their reactions. If the new topic is too far removed from their experiences they may become confused. If they do, stop the discussion, clear up their confusion, and then continue.

- If the others are interested in the general subject area you want to discuss, again move ahead. For example, if you're with a group of guys who are interested in engines and all have tinkered around with their cars, chances are they would also be curious about how a jet engine works. But don't let the conversation get too technical; keep it restricted to simple explanations such as "air comes in the forward end, where it's compressed in the compressor section. Next it's mixed with fuel and ignited in burner cans. The hot gases then turn the turbines as they expand toward the rear exhaust." You wouldn't want to discuss the difference between the first, second and third stages of the compressor; this would be getting too detailed and complex. In other words, keep the conversation simple *unless* the others make it clear that they want to dig more deeply into the subject.

- If some of the group members have no experience or interest in the new topic and some do, then consider using two new topics to start two separate discussions. When the two conversations start to slow down, then bring everyone back into one single conversation.

The key, then, to keeping your listeners attentive so they enjoy conversing with you is to steer the conversation toward a topic that ties into their interests, their education level or their personal experience.

WHEN IT PAYS YOU TO BE RIGHT

"It doesn't pay to be right all the time!" I often make this statement to someone just to see what reaction I'll get. And the reaction usually can be summed up in one of these statements:

- "No human is ever always right."
- "I hate people who *act* as if they're always right . . . who never admit they've made a mistake."

No one will ever feel this way about you as long as you keep putting yourself in the other person's place and conversing from his point of view. If you do this and you make a mistake, you'll admit it right away rather than trying to act as if the mistake didn't happen. Or if you offend someone you'll apologize immediately. So you can make mistakes and still be a respected conversationalist.

But there is one time when it's distinctly to your advantage to be correct and to avoid mistakes. This is when you want to motivate someone else into doing something you want him to do. Since motivating others requires specialized conversational techniques, we'll spend a chapter on it later in the book. But for now, let's discuss two important timing factors you will want to use when motivating others:

First, be sure you have complete information . . .

Assume you work in a large office and one day you notice two clerks gathering printed papers and stapling them together. You recall that you've seen them collating papers like this before. So you ask a few questions and discover that each girl collates for about two hours a day . . . that a total of four hours a day, 20 hours a week, 80 hours a month. So you march into your boss's office and proudly announce: "I've got an idea that will save us a lot of time and money. I have been watching the girls stapling printed sheets together. If we bought an automatic collating machine, one person could do all this work. And she'd probably do it in less than half the 80 hours a month it takes us now."

That's quite a saving," your boss answers. "Give me all the facts."

"What would you like to know?" you ask, as you start taking the following notes:

- How many hours would we really save?
- Based on our labor cost per hour, how much money would we save?
- How much would a collator cost?
- How long would it take before our cost savings equaled the cost of the collator machine?

You leave your boss' office with mixed feelings . . . you had a good idea and you thought you could score some points with him; and it's true, you did show him that you're alert and looking for ways to help him save money. But you also showed him a weakness . . . you spoke up without first having all the facts.

You won't often face situations as complex as this example, but you can learn from the principle involved: Have correct and complete information *before* you start a conversation intended to motivate someone else, and you'll have a much better chance of succeeding.

Be sure you are talking to the right person . . .

I recall a story told to me by Sam Smatters. One day he received a letter forwarded from his home office . . . John Johansen, Plant Engineer for Veronly Manufacturing, wanted information about the new Model 75 lathe. "A good sale lead, this one," thought Sam. So he started gathering information by talking to other salesmen who had called on John Johansen and by reading his own company's literature on the good points of the Model 75. When Sam called on John, he had the information he needed to motivate John into buying.

The sales interview went well and Sam got John to agree that Veronly should purchase a new Model 75. Two weeks later, he called on John again to get a written purchase order and was told, "Sorry, but all machines costing as much as yours must be bought by the Plant Superintendent. He's been talking to your competitor and plans to buy from him."

Sam explained to me, "I lost the sale because I missed one key fact when gathering information . . . the other salesmen I talked to sold lower-priced items that John could buy on his own authority." Whether or not you are a salesman, the principle of this example still holds true: when you wish to motivate others make sure you're talking to the person who has the power to cause the conversation to turn out as you want it to.

In summary, it doesn't always pay to be right . . . be human, you can hurt your reputation as a conversationalist if you act as if you're always correct. But there is one time when you should try your best to be correct, and that's when you are trying to motivate someone else.

KEYING INTO THE CONVERSATIONAL CLIMATE

I'm sure you've noticed how different plants and flowers need the right climate if they are to grow and thrive . . . palm trees need year-round warmth and moisture . . . impatiens flowers in warm shade . . . while the iris prefers fairly sunny spots.

Conversation, too, thrives best when the climate is right. That's why it's always to your advantage when you join a new conversational group first, to determine the climate existing in the group, and second, to be sure you key into this climate.

Discovering a group's conversational climate

Conversational climate is simply the mood or general feeling of a group:

- It can be happy and jovial. Example: a party held for a football team that just won a major game.
- It can be serious. Example: a group of students comparing notes before a big test.
- It can be worried or apprehensive. Example: a meeting of employees of a defense-oriented company which just lost a big government contract.
- It can be bored. Example: a group of basically quiet people who have exhausted all the topics they had to talk about.
- It can be tired. Example: a group of women who have just finished running a day-long church fair.

Discovering a group's conversational climate is best done by listening and observing before you speak. About two seconds' listening is all you need to spot a jovial group or a serious one. Worried or bored people often wear their feelings on their faces. And it doesn't take much time to spot the weary, bedraggled look of a tired group.

Conversing in tune with the climate

Once you've noted a groups' prevailing climate, you can easily take a conversational approach in tune with the groups' feelings:

- If you join a jovial group, relax and join in the fun with comments such as, "Hey, Joe, that was a great catch you made on the ten-yard line. It looked to me as if the other team almost intercepted. Did their linebacker touch the ball before you?"
- If you join a group holding a serious discussion, simply keep quiet until you have something positive to add. If they're college students preparing for a test on the major sources of food for farm animals, you would be safely in the right climate if you remark, "I've heard that the two biggest sources of protein-rich animal feed are American-grown soybeans and anchovies fished from Peruvian coastal waters."

- If you join a group of workers worried about possible layoffs, jokes definitely would not be appreciated.
- But don't hesitate to use your jokes to liven up a bored group.
- Finally, a tired group of workers would have the most respect for your conversational insight if you quickly observed their worn-out look and asked, "I know I just got here, but is there anything I can do to help clean up?"

Keying into the conversational climate is much like swimming with friends at a salt-water beach. When the tide is coming in strong, there's an undertow that's hard to fight; it can carry you away from your friends on the shore if you're not careful . . . but there are also incoming waves that, if your timing is right, will carry you easily and quickly right back to your friends on the beach.

Conversing in a way that's out of tune with the conversational climate is like being caught in an undertow . . . you'll find yourself being swept away from your friends on the beach . . . or simply away from the mainstream of the conversation. But keying into the climate is like riding a wave towards shore . . . you will automatically be carried closer to friends . . . you will be accepted into the conversation.

BREAKING UP DEADLOCKS

At one time or another, you'll be caught in a situation where the others involved disagree with each other and no one is willing to change his mind. When this happens, you're stuck with a deadlocked conversation, a go-nowhere discussion. Two of the more common causes of deadlocks are these:

- *Differences of opinion.* During the annual November election campaign, for example, opinions naturally differ. If resulting political discussions are open-minded and objective, fine. But conversations often become deadlocked:
  "How can you be so stupid! Elect Larry and

he'll turn this town into a shambles with his crazy
ideas."

"Yeh, that's what you say. I say elect Sam and
we'll have four do-nothing years."

When a conversation turns into a go-nowhere
hassle, then break the deadlock. In the above example, the timing would be perfect for a statement
such as:

"Let's talk politics after the election. We all
have our own opinions and no one's going to
change. So let's get onto a more agreeable subject
where we're not growling at each other."

In fact, you should even go a step further and
suggest a new topic:

"Next month is our club's big dinner dance.
We still have to decide on what decorations to
use. I suggest . . ."

• *Conflicts of interest.* In a business conversation, for
example, the sales manager may complain that he
can't get enough sales because "the product's cost is
too high." The pricing manager may respond that he
can't lower prices "until manufacturing costs come
down." The manufacturing manager argues that
costs are high because he's being forced to produce
a product that is "too high in quality." And, finally,
the quality control manager answers that "our
quality isn't high enough . . . I'm getting too many
customer complaints about our products now."

In this conversation everyone has a valid point of
view, but each sees the problem from a limited point
of view. Somebody has to take the overall view and
resolve each person's problems . . . and that somebody might as well be you. So you might remark:

"I think you each have a point, but we'll need
more facts before we can solve this problem. Why
don't we break up our meeting for now, and I'll
get back to each of you later with an answer."

You then could privately ask the quality control

manager, "What exactly are our customers complaining about?" Then, armed with this information, you and the manufacturing manager can decide where to cut corners and where to keep quality high. The end result will be lower cost and thus the lower price the sales manager needs. I know this technique works because I've seen it used quite often by a highly successful engineering vice-president. Use this method yourself, and it won't be long before your boss regards you as a man worth promoting.

While the conversational techniques you use to break deadlocked conversations will vary with the situation, one timing fact never varies . . . and that is this: when a conversation deadlocks, nothing can be gained by letting it continue. In fact, discussion often makes the deadlock worse . . . each person just digs in more deeply and becomes more committed to his opinion. By switching the conversation to a different subject you give the people a chance to calm down. If the topic is an important one, you can always come back to it later . . . after tempers have cooled and the others are in a more open-minded mood. In the meantime see if you can change the subject . . . or find a different way to approach the problem . . . or find a compromise that recognizes all points of view . . . or find a way that lets someone give in and change his opinion without losing face. By choosing one of these timing actions, you'll bring peace back into the conversation. And you'll soon find people complimenting you for your calming influence and cool head.

6

Awakening Your Senses So They Add Sparkle to Your Conversation

Now that the basic conversational skills of talking and listening are becoming a natural part of your personality, you're ready to add an extra dimension that sought-after conversationalists have in common . . . their talk sparkles with lively thoughts and words . . . their enthusiasm is contagious . . . when they're present conversations are much more interesting, much more alive and vital. A major cause of this liveliness is that wide-awake conversationalists tune their five senses into the world around them and then use what their senses note to add vitality to their conversation. Everyone was born with the ability to see, hear, feel, smell and taste, but not everyone fully uses these senses. Try the following experiment; it's designed to help you discover how fully you are using your senses:

Assume that it's fall and you're living in the north-eastern United States. Form mental pictures of what your surroundings are like. Let your imagination run wild . . . make these mental images as vivid and specific as possible . . . use as many of your senses as you can. Then take paper and pencil and write down how you would describe these mental images to a friend in conversation.

Now read over your description and note how many times you used one of your senses in describing the mental pictures you had created. Did you write, "I *saw* two trees right next to each other, one with rust-colored leaves and the other with bright gold leaves. What a beautiful contrast they made." Or, "I *felt* a cool, brisk wind blow falling leaves against my face." Or,

"I *heard* fallen leaves rustle and crunch under my feet as I walked."

Next note how often you used your five senses by listing "see, hear, feel, smell and taste" down the left side of a paper; then put a check mark next to a sense each time you used it in the description.

Finally total the check marks. If you used each sense more than three times you are above average. Congratulations, your senses are most surely wide awake. Most people who try this experiment are surprised when they learn how sparingly they use all their senses. Yet, if they were to waken their senses and put them to work, they'd be amazed at how much more enjoyable their lives would become. Each new happening would take on added depth and meaning . . . they would both see and smell a flower . . . feel and hear a breeze . . . taste and smell a glass of grape juice. And this depth would help them to put more excitement into their conversation. For example, which of these sets of remarks would be more interesting to listen to?

- Someone remarks about a flower:
  "Looks pretty."
  "Isn't it beautiful the way each petal gracefully curves up and out?"
- Someone remarks about a breeze:
  "Oh, it's cool."
  "Listen to the pretty sound as the breeze ripples the top of the bushes."
- Someone remarks about a glass of grape juice:
  "Tastes good."
  "I love that fresh-fruit smell. It seems to make the drink taste better."

Wide-awake senses are so vital to good conversation that the rest of this chapter will examine each sense individually.

HOW YOUR EYES CAN LIVEN UP
YOUR CONVERSATION

"**Run Spot run.**"
"**See Spot run.**"

Just about every first grader reads sentences like these two. They describe a skim-the-surface type of seeing that is perfectly okay for youngsters. But as people grow into adulthood, their sense of vision should also grow until they use it to see and to converse on a much higher level.

Continuing with the first-grade reader example, take the statement, "See Spot." It's a pretty bland thing to say . . . it really adds nothing to a conversation other than to point out that a dog is nearby.

Making better use of your vision. This can easily be done simply by noting in detail what the dog is doing. If he's running, you could say,

"See Spot run."

Or, better still you could say,

"See how fast and gracefully Spot runs."

Or, even better yet,

"Look at the way Spot is chasing that rabbit. He runs so fast, yet changes direction so easily whenever the rabbit zigs or zags. And despite his speed and turns, he's still graceful and beautiful to watch."

It's obvious that the last statement is the most interesting. The major difference between the first and last statement is not what Spot did . . . the difference is the way you used your vision sense to increase the quality of your conversation.

Put yourself in your listener's shoes for a minute. The first statement wasn't very exciting; it would have given you, the listener, the feeling that you were hearing a lackluster remark. The second comment has enough interest to it that I'm sure you'd take a moment to watch Spot. But the third remark would tell you what to watch for . . . you would start admiring Spot's gracefulness along with the speaker. You would feel a moment of companionship as you enjoyed the sight together . . . his excellent use of his vision sense, combined with a well-worded remark, would bring you closer together.

Good use of the vision sense certainly is a strong contributor to powerful and lively conversation.

Using understanding to add conversational depth. As you become more adept at using your vision sense to its fullest, you'll find it'll add an extra dimension of depth to your conversations.

For example, if you were to keep watching Spot, you'd eventually observe Spot playing with his ten-year-old master, Alan . . . you'd note how Spot would "play bite" on Alan's arm . . . how Spot's large jaws would encircle the boys flesh, yet not close hard enough to even leave a tooth mark. In the same play period you would note how Spot rolls over, exposing his underbelly to Alan . . . you'd know from previous experience that an animal never willingly moves into such an unprotected position unless he feels perfectly safe from harm. By noting these two actions you'd be in an ideal position to comment:

"Isn't it wonderful the way Alan and Spot trust each other? Spot's jaws are powerful enough to crush Alan's arm, yet his play bite doesn't leave a mark. And Spot trusts Alan so completely that he rolls over and exposes his soft underbelly to Alan. Could you see Spot doing that in a dogfight?"

Good conversationalists have long used their vision sense to add to a conversation's interest. I can remember a very interesting discussion I once had with George Reade. George had noted a dog and his young master asleep on the same bed at night. He observed how the youngster had crawled far into the bed's corner to make room for the dog. This scene provided the raw material for our conversation on how a boy-dog relationship helps teach a boy to love and to share.

Making yourself a more reliable conversationalist. Many people talk about what they see. But, remember that old party game where you watch two people do something, then everyone takes turns describing what he saw? It's amazing how much the descriptions can differ. This problem of selective observation is all too familiar to policemen who must try to make sense out of conflicting comments they receive from eye witnesses to a crime.

Selective observation occurs when your mind plays tricks with your observations. It's a problem that you must overcome if you want others to look up to you as a reliable conversationalist.

Selective observation is a very natural misuse of the vision sense. Though your eyes see everything in sight, your mind oftentimes accepts only those observations it wants to accept.

For example, when I owned a Chevrolet, I usually noticed other Chevrolets I passed on the road and ignored other types of cars. Then I bought a Ford and suddenly my "observations" changed . . . I now saw as many Fords as Chevrolets. In fact, I even reached the point where I started to "observe" more Fords than Chevrolets. But I knew this couldn't be true . . . the ratio of Fords to Chevrolets just doesn't change that quickly; so one morning, I decided to make a careful count of the Fords and Chevrolets I saw on my way to work. I counted three Chevrolets, then saw a Ford. My "observations" up to that point told me that I had seen Chevrolets in a ratio of 3 to 1 over Fords. Then I noticed an interesting fact: the car sitting right next to the Ford was a Chevrolet that I had not included in my count.

At some time or another your mind will also play this kind of trick with your vision . . . it will edit your observations and note only what it wants to see. So learn to observe accurately and objectively and your conversations will automatically be accurate . . . your listeners will look up to you as a reliable conversationalist.

HOW OPENING YOUR EARS LETS IN A
WORLD OF CONVERSATIONAL MATERIAL

The same principle holds true for hearing as for visio. . . . the degree of "color" and liveliness your hearing sense adds to your conversation depends on how well you use it. For example, everyone notes a sound when it occurs . . . or do they?

- How often have you heard the birds singing in the trees as you wake up in the morning and then used this fact to make an interesting breakfast comment to your wife?
- How often has your mind been completely focused on a thought when suddenly you realize that someone is talking to you . . . and has been for quite a few minutes?

There are many things that cause our hearing sense to turn off . . . the high level of noise existing in our world today is one reason . . . the fast-paced life we live is another . . . and the fact that we've trained ourselves to concentrate hard on the job at hand is a third cause. But whatever the reason, the fact remains that most people simply don't note every sound that occurs; and thus they can't gain any conversational advantage from these sounds.

Selecting the sounds worth listening to. If you paid complete attention to every sound that occurred around you, your life would soon become too sound-filled for comfort . . . furthermore, you'd never have time in a 24-hour day to comment on every sound. So you must decide which sounds to tune out and which ones to tune in.

Experienced conversationalists do this first by becoming aware that a sound has occurred, then by asking themselves, "Is this sound important enough to pay attention to?" For example, the sounds of a passing car or a far-off dog barking can be ignored safely. But an immediate comment to your wife is demanded by the sounds of a car pulling into your driveway or by your own dog barking at 1:00 AM.

Once you're aware of a sound and you've decided to tune it in, you can use conversation to search for its meaning. Connie and Red Stevens did this when they heard their seven-year old daughter crying. Red automatically asked Connie, "Is that the make-believe cry she uses when playing with her dolls, or did she hurt herself?" The tone of her cry quickly gave Connie her answer, "It's O.K. She's just playing." Short conversations such as this help develop a feeling of closeness and family interest between husband and wife.

Using the mental image technique. The sounds you hear add the most life to your conversation only if you use them to form mental pictures and then base your conversation on these mental images.

When you prepared a description of fall in the Northeast, here are two statements you could have made:

- "I heard the scraping sound of rakes pushing fallen leaves into great big piles."

● "And, I heard happy laughter as young children played in the huge leaf piles."

Raking and laughter . . . two different sounds, yet when they're put together in a mental picture, they form the makings of some conversational comments well worth listening to . . . comments that will add color to your conversation and make you a much more interesting person to listen to.

Here's another example of how open ears provide good conversational material. While at a party one October Saturday night, I was talking with Rolf Jenkins. He remarked about the local high school football game we had both attended that afternoon: "Wasn't it fun to sit in the stands and cheer for our hometown team?"

"It certainly was," I answered. But I didn't say more because I instinctively felt that Rolf had more he wanted to say.

"When I heard all the yelling and cheering, I looked around in the stands . . . it was surprising . . . Jack and his son Tom were sitting together and enjoying the game; and Larry and his son Eric were yelling so loud they must be hoarse tonight. You know, that's the first time in a long while that I've seen either Jack or Larry agreeing with his son . . . usually they're at each other's throats. Isn't it interesting how a common interest can wipe away the generation gap?"

Yes, your hearing sense can add great liveliness and "color" to your conversation when you open it to the world around you and then consciously use it to gather material that will enrich your conversation.

HOW TO PRODUCTIVELY USE YOUR SENSE OF TOUCH

How often do you touch something but do not feel it? More often than you think, I'd bet. That's why I'd like you to take this quickie test:

1. Describe the feel of your car's steering wheel after a long drive on a hot summer day.
2. When you last put on your winter overcoat, how did the material feel? Smooth? Furry? Rough? Or

woolly?

3. Last night how did your pajamas feel as they
   rubbed against your skin? Like a blend of cotton
   and synthetic? Like all cotton? Or like all synthetic?

Most people have to think pretty hard when they try this
quickie test. They don't immediately recall the feel of their
overcoat and pajamas. And many forget the slightly stickly
feeling of a steering wheel after a long drive on a hot day.

The majority of people "fail" this test for one simple
reason ... practically every minute of every day they are
touching something. It's simply impossible to react to every
sensation that their skin is exposed to. So it's only natural
they'll ignore most of them. While ignoring sensations is natural,
it isn't ideal ... as is true for your vision and hearing sense,
your sense of touch also can add depth and interest to your
conversations. The solution to this problem: Be selective;
carefully pick and choose which sensations you'll ignore. It's
amazing, however, that most sensations people tend to ignore
are the very sensations that can add to their conversational
ability.

For example, let's go back to Question Three about
pajamas in the quickie test. Not long ago Jim Bennett used a
question much like this to solve a problem. His wife had asked,
"Jim, your pajamas are wearing out too fast. Do you have any
idea why?"

He thought awhile, and then remembered: "I think they
started wearing out faster around the time they took on a less
silky feel."

"A less silky feel? Oh, I know what you mean. I used to
buy a brand of pajamas that were a cotton and synthetic blend.
Lately I've been buying 100% cotton ones."

Maybe that's the problem," Jim responded. "Have you
noticed which type you've been throwing away?"

Now it was his wife's turn to mentally review the feel of
various fabrics. "I believe it was the 100% cotton ones."

Result of this conversation: The Bennetts now buy cot-
ton/synthetic-blend pajamas and the problem has disappeared.

Although in this example the sense of touch didn't produce a long conversation, it certainly led to a productive one.

The sense of touch doesn't restrict you only to conversations about physical things. It can lead to interesting and colorful conversations including descriptive comments, such as this one a friend of mine made one October: "The air was so cold that it almost seemed to slap my face when I walked out to the car this morning."

It also can produce conversations where you prove your sensitivity toward others by making a comment such as: "I felt quick, loving kisses on my lips this morning as our family headed in different directions . . . I to work, the kids to school and Mommy back to the breakfast table to eat the meal she didn't have time for until the others left."

Comments like the last one show how the sense of touch is often a wordless conversation in itself. If your house is anything like mine, mornings are busy. But despite the rush and hurry, there's always time for a quick, yet loving kiss goodbye. It only takes a moment, but it says, "I love you. I want only the best for you today."

It's true that feeling something contacting your skin is the sense that you experience most often. Thus it's a goldmine of conversational material. You can describe the feel of pants as they rub against your legs and sleeves against your arms . . . you can describe to your friend how sore your muscles feel from the work you did over the weekend . . . and as your hands constantly touch one item or another, you can discuss their roughness or smoothness, heat or cold and so on. But because you touch and feel so many things every day, it's simply impossible to discuss every one of these sensations. On the other hand, you want to use your sense of touch whenever possible as a source of comments to liven up your conversation. So, as mentioned above, the trick is to be selective in choosing which touch sensations to explore and discuss to their fullest. This is done easily by discussing those sensations which have the greatest interest for your listeners. In this way you automatically use a strong natural ability to add life and sparkle to your conversations.

HOW TO USE YOUR SENSE OF SMELL
TO ENRICH CONVERSATIONS

While your sense of touch is stimulated very often, your sense of smell isn't used anywhere near as frequently. Thus, chances are you'll be more apt to note new stimuli as they occur. Smells can have varying degrees of intensity:

- *Scent* is the most delicate. It is the faint new-car smell you can still detect in a year-old auto . . . it is the faint perfume you notice on your wife at the end of an evening out.
- *Odor* is more readily noticed: it is the smell of a one-month-old car, or perfume newly applied.
- *Aroma* occurs when a smell is more penetrating yet still pleasant. It's an aroma that greets you when you enter your home and smell a roast cooking.

Almost everyone notes an odor or an aroma, while a scent is noticed by some and ignored by others. A good conversationalist, however, is sensitive to any smell, regardless of its intensity. Your wife, for example, would be flattered if you remarked to her, "What a lovely perfume you're wearing. I've been enjoying it all evening."

And many conversationalists have learned how to use the sense of smell as a form of wordless conversation. Take the case of Mrs. Reade, who had a breakfast-time argument with her husband, George. When he arrived home that evening, he noted a delicious aroma coming from the kitchen. He further sensed that what he smelled was leg of lamb stuffed with garlic. This is his favorite roast, although his wife prefers lamb cooked without garlic. The meaning is clear; his wife is saying, "I'm sorry we quarreled this morning." It seems that Mrs. Reade is as astute a conversationalist as her husband George. That's probably why they have so many good friends who always seek out their company.

HOW YOUR TONGUE'S TASTE SENSE
IMPROVES ITS SPEAKING ABILITY

There are many words and phrases you can use conversationally to distinguish one taste from another. For example, food can be bland or highly seasoned . . . it can have a delicate flavor or be penetrating and tangy. Once you start to distinguish between these various taste sensations and comment about them, then you are relating one taste to another . . . you are using your sense of taste to add to the interest and breadth of your conversation.

And the sense of taste is quite frequently used as a method of gathering people together so they can enjoy good conversation. I can remember from my bachelor days how a group of us would gather weekly at a restaurant known for its tasty meals. While we enjoyed our food, we'd engage in animated and stimulating conversation about political and social issues of the day. Many good friendships were formed as a result of these conversations . . . conversations that never would have taken place without the excuse of a shared dinner to bring us together.

You often can go beyond using just your taste sense . . . you can combine your senses of taste, touch and smell. Take the favorite men's meal—corned beef and cabbage. Imagine a steaming bowl of it sitting smack in the middle of your dining room table. Smell it in your mind. Taste the salty beef mingling with the bland cabbage. Feel the different textures of crumbly beef and smooth cabbage rubbing against your tongue. Whoever invented this meal certainly knew how to give a fellow pleasure through a mixed appeal to his senses . . . a pleasure that undoubtedly will lead to many complimentary conversational comments.

Most women understand this trick of combining taste sensations and use this knowledge every day to help plan their menus. In fact, many wives use food as a wordless conversation . . . by preparing meals they know their family likes, they are really saying, "I love you all. I want you to eat, to enjoy, to be happy."

The sense of taste often sparks a spoken conversation as

well. I can remember Blanche Archer describing "the taste of newly-squeezed cider made by an old cider press at the annual Country Fair." Her description of the taste led, in turn, to a conversation comparing the way we live today with the way people lived when cider was first made. What an interesting conversation that one was! We all came away from it with a much greater appreciation of the ease and comfort of our lives today. But we also felt a certain sadness for the slower pace of living we sacrificed to obtain our current comforts.

The previous conversation started with a discussion of a taste sensation, then developed into a broader conversation that helped everyone present gain a momentary sense of perspective on the quality of his living. It's just one more example of how it pays to wake up your senses . . . of how using your senses to their fullest will surely add liveliness, depth and interest to your conversation.

7

Building a Knowledge Reservoir That Never Lets Your Conversation Run Dry

You can't escape from talk; it's all around you . . . on your job, in your home, at social gatherings. But unfortunately much of this talk is say-nothing, time-killing noise. For instance, read this discussion between Tony and Gary . . .

Tony: "Sure was a mess getting to work today."
Gary: "Traffic bad?"
Tony: "Slow, slow, slow."
Gary: "Yeh, I've been in tie ups, too. They're a pain."

. . . now compare the above with this conversation between Larry and Scott

Larry: "Boy was the Expressway backed up today . . . stop-and-go all the way from Exit 9 to Exit 13."
Scott: "Yeh, I know that stretch . . . get a little snow on the big hill and traffic slows to a walk."
Larry: "That's what happened! And to make it worse, a truck jackknifed half way up the hill."
Scott: "What a mess that must have been."

It's obvious that the first discussion is uninspiring, dry and boring, while Larry and Scott are having meaningful conversation . . . it is enjoyable and interesting. The difference: The second is loaded with facts and information. These two vital ingredients separate say-nothing talk from meaningful conversation. Build these ingredients into your discussions and people will seek you out when they feel like enjoying a worthwhile conversation.

And you can count on facts and information popping almost magically into your mind when you need them if you prepare a little bit ahead of time. Just as a city digs reservoirs to store the water its people will need for the future, you also can prepare a reservoir . . . a mental reservoir stocked with the knowledge that will assure many meaningful and enjoyable conversations.

CHOOSING THE INFORMATION BEST FOR YOU

The easiest way to fill your knowledge reservoir is by becoming both a generalist and a specialist. When you want work done around the house, you can call in a general handyman or many specialists. If, for example, your faucet leaks, your bathroom wallpaper needs repasting and your grass is overgrown, you probably would call in a general handyman. None of these jobs requires highly skilled labor.

On the other hand, if you need new kitchen plumbing, new bathroom wallpaper and a relandscaping job, it would be far wiser—and much more efficient—to call in a plumber, a wallpaperer and a gardener.

The same is true for conversation. During an average month you will converse with many people. Some conversations will require a general handyman's reservoir of knowledge, others a specialist's:

- Since most of the time you'll be talking with people you don't know very well, it's helpful to have a general knowledge about many topics. This greatly increases your chances of sparking interesting discussions with casual acquaintances, thus increasing your reputation as a good conversationalist.
- When you're with closer friends, your conversations will dig fairly deeply into specific topics. To keep

these conversations lively you'll need the more extensive knowledge of a specialist.

Thus, you'll come out ahead if your knowledge reservoir is both broad in scope and deep in a few specific areas.

HOW TO STOCK A GENERALIST'S RESERVOIR

Though you'll want a general knowledge of many subjects, there's a limit to the number of topics on which you can develop enough working knowledge to keep an interesting conversation alive.

Here's a technique many conversationalists use to choose which topics they will learn about ... basically the technique boils down to limiting yourself to subjects that interest the largest number of your casual acquaintances. Here's how it works.

First, divide a piece of paper into three columns ... in column one list five to ten people whom you see fairly often, in column two write their major interests, and in column three note their minor interests. At the end, put your own interests. For example:

1 Individual's Name	2 Major Interests	3 Minor Interests
Bill	Football	Woodworking
Charley	Baseball	Drawing
Sam	Handicrafts	Poker
Dick	Bridge	Football
Scott	Sculpting and painting	Basketball
Your Interests	Puttering and making things for the home	Football

Second, glance over the listing and look for interests the people have in common. As a guide, here is one way you could analyze these listings:

1. What is a general interest these people share in common? Answer: Sports. All but Sam are inter-

ested in fast-moving spectator sports. And since these are well-organized sports, they are richly laden with conversational material on which you can draw: league standings, upcoming games, outstanding players, predictions of league winners, and so on.

2. What is another common interest? Answer: Creative arts and hobbies. Woodworking, drawing, sculpturing, handicrafts, and making things for the home are all hobbies requiring creativity. If these were your acquaintances, it would be to your advantage to learn about their hobbies. Then you'd always have the knowledge you'd need to hold their interest when you converse with them. And you'd also win their gratitude since you could praise them knowledgeably whenever they create something outstanding.

So the way to become a generalist is to list the topics that interest the people with whom you frequently converse, and then to study the listings for common interests that lead to enjoyable conversations such as this one Jim Everett had:

"Hi, Jim, did you see the playoff game yesterday?"
"I sure did. And UCLA was playing much better than they did in the semi-finals. Remember when . . ."

Build your generalist's reservoir. Not only will other people enjoy talking with you, but you will also gain more pleasure from your conversations. Psychologists have discovered that the more you know about a topic, the more you will become interested in that topic . . . and as your interest and knowledge grow, so will your enjoyment.

WHEN AND HOW TO SPECIALIZE

Recall the analogy given above: If you had a leaky faucet, peeling wallpaper and overgrown grass, you would call in a general handyman. But if you needed new kitchen plumbing, new wallpaper and relandscaping, you would engage three specialists . . . a plumber, a wallpaper hanger and a gardener.

By listing the interests of many casual acquaintances, you have pinpointed topics where it would pay you to build a generalist's reservoir of facts and information. You have not wasted your time and energy in unproductive areas; rather you have obtained only useful knowledge. You've made good progress . . . if you stopped right now you'd have a wider knowledge reservoir and thus be a better conversationalist. But why be satisfied with a job only half-done?

Consider a wide, yet shallow, lake. It isn't a full-fledged reservoir, since once its few feet of water is removed, only dry and barren ground remains. But make the lake deeper, and it becomes a reliable water supply because its storage capacity is now much greater. The same is true for conversation . . . a knowledge reservoir, like one for water, must be deep as well as broad if it's to help you greatly improve your conversational ability.

Where should you seek knowledge in depth? In what topics should you specialize? It all depends on your personality and your interests . . . some of the many possibilities from which you can choose are given in the following pages.

Drawing riches from your environment

It's a fact that your life is influenced greatly by your environment, by the area where you live and by people you contact daily. So it makes sense to draw from your environment; it's a rich source of information you can use to build a specialist's reservoir. For example, here are just three knowledge sources your environment provides.

Your job is a wellspring of information . . .

You work eight hours per day, five days a week, spending one-third of your week-day hours on the job. And you're not alone . . . millions of other people do exactly the same thing. It follows naturally, then, that most people would be interested in talking about their work and in learning about the work that other people do. This leads to two topics where you can pick up special knowledge that'll improve your conversational ability: the work you do, and the product your company makes.

It's easy to talk about the work you do . . . after all, you are automatically building up the knowledge reservoir you'll need during the forty hours you spend on the job every week.

But what about the product your company makes . . . it must have interest and value, or no one would buy it. So start asking questions and find out as much as you can about it. How did it come to be discovered or invented? How is it made? How is it used? What advantages does it have over similar products? Such questions not only help you build your knowledge reservoir, but they also make your job much more meaningful. And they make you a more interesting conversationalist. For example, do you think Tom or Al does a better job of conversing if you asked him, "You work at XYZ Company? I've often passed your plant . . . what do you make?"

Tom: "Some type of radio device for ships. I'm not sure what it does."

Al: "A radio directional finder for boat owners. Suppose you were boating out in the middle of the bay and a fog rolled in. You would quickly lose your sense of direction, so you would turn on our directional finder and. . . ."

Your co-workers are another knowledge source . . .

Your job also brings you into daily contact with your co-workers, all of whom have interests of their own. At lunch time and at coffee break, they talk about topics that interest them. As they do, you surely can pick up new knowledge. In fact, talking with others is such a rich source of information that we'll discuss it under another topic that follows shortly.

Your geographical area is yet another information source . . .

Your environment also includes that part of the physical world that you contact in your everyday living . . . your home, the town where you live, the county where your town is located, the state, the United States. Each of these locations is a rich source of useful conversational material.

For example, let's choose the home-town location and see how others have used it to build a specialist's reservoir. I grew up in Rockville Centre, a commuters' suburb located about 20 miles from New York City on the south shore of Long Island. While I have often heard people base conversations on this town, one incident stands out in my mind.

At a Kiwanis dinner meeting, I unsuccessfully tried many times to draw quiet and reserved Art Johnson out of his shell. Then another of the group mentioned Art's interest in local history, and grasping at this cue, I encouraged him to talk about his interest. It worked: For a fascinating hour, Art told of one historical incident after another with all the enthusiasm of a professional teller of tales:

- "Did you know our town was once a major Indian wampum center?"
- "And Rockville Centre saw the first blood shed on Long Island during the Revolution. Loyalists hid by day in the woods bordering Malverne, then fled southward at night to the swamps where Woodmere is now. Revolutionaries searching the woods for these Loyalists ran into a group of them. The resulting skirmish caused the first blood to be spilled."

Because of his knowledge reservoir about local history, Art was transformed from a conversational wallflower into the center of attention. Yes, having specialized knowledge can help you put life and interest into mostly any conversation. And your environment is one sure source of information you can use in adding depth to your knowledge reservoir.

YOUR FRIENDS—A NATURAL GOLD MINE

Finding things to talk about with your close friends presents no problem . . . you share many common interests and experiences with them. But trouble comes when your conversations center only on experiences you have shared in the past. For example:

You are comfortably seated in your friend's living room and the conversation is just starting to pick up steam. Then your friend remarks, "Remember that

time we took the gals on the boat, 'Albatros', for a day-long fishing trip?" At that point you settle back resignedly for the umpteenth rehashing of this ten-year-old incident.

Friendships can grow stale, conversations uninteresting and your reputation as a conversationalist disappear unless new topics are introduced every now and then . . . new topics that will arouse everyone's interest and once again put life and enthusiasm into your discussions. There are two ways to develop these topic areas: a give and a take.

You can take topics . . .

. . . in which your friend is very interested and develop knowledge of your own in these areas.

Let's assume your friend is a coin collector. Although you don't have to start your own collection, you can read a book or two about the hobby. Then when you're with your friend, his ears most certainly will pick up when you comment, "I read yesterday that a 1913 Liberty head nickel is now worth twice as much as a $2.50 gold piece." Chances are he will respond to your newly-shown interest by telling you more about the coins he has and why he values them. After a few such conversations your knowledge of coin collecting will surely become deep enough for you to hold you own easily in future talks on the subject. And your friend will certainly look forward to his next meeting with you.

To *take* a friend's interest and learn more about it is a passive approach to conversation . . . you will listen more than you will talk.

If you prefer a more active role, then you should *give*.

When giving, pick a topic . . .

. . . that is similar to your friend's interest, yet different. Let's go back to your coin collecting friend. The personality traits required to enjoy this hobby include a desire to own something that not everybody has . . . a willingness to spend time studying about a specific hobby . . . and a quiet nature that finds joy in solitary mental stimulation. If you were to pick a topic that appeals to these personality traits, you surely would hold his interest in conversation.

Suppose your friend worked as a research scientist and relaxed after hours by creating modern oil paintings. With this combination of talents, chances are strong that he would enjoy an animated discussion on what it would be like to travel to other planets ... this subject would give both his creative imagination and his scientific interest plenty of room in which to roam.

Or perhaps your friend is a home improvement buff. Here you have a wealth of topics ... furniture refinishing, decorating ideas and landscaping schemes are just three.

The interests of your friends provide a natural gold mine of topics from which you can deepen your knowledge reservoir. Study up on them. Then *give* or *take* ... either way will surely add more life to your friendships and will make your conversation more enriching for everyone.

Using a colorful personality as an extra plus

There are many similarities between color and personality. For example, you see many different colors in a normal week ... five, twenty-five, a hundred and fifty-five, sometimes even more. Specifically, you probably saw many shades of blue yesterday ... French blue, powder blue, royal blue, turquoise blue, sky blue, navy blue ... the list could go on and on. Yet despite all the colors that exist, each one has a personality of its own ... by choosing the proper color you can give a room a restful warmth, an invigorating freshness, or an aloof coolness. And I'm sure you've noticed how certain colors are so appealing that they are used again and again ... on walls, in clothes, on cars.

The same is true for the human personality ... there are millions upon millions of different personalities, yet certain ones have more appeal than others. I'm sure you know many people whose personalities are so spontaneous and so pleasantly appealing that you automatically give them center stage when conversing. What is so appealing about these people? Once you know the answer, you will be able to use it to put color into your conversations. So as you read the following case histories, keep asking yourself this question ... "Why is this fellow's personality appealing?"

- Raised on a Midwest farm, Sy Rhones had a happy childhood full of rich experiences . . . fishing from a country brook using a fresh-cut tree sapling as a rod . . . eating corn plucked fresh from its stalk and dropped right into a boiling kettle . . . taking hunting trips with Dad for coon and possum . . . spending long winter evenings listening to old timers' tales of what used to be. Memories of his youth are so strong for Sy, that he often fills his conversation with references to the "good old farm days." And when he is in the right mood, his very expressions and method of talking have such a strong hay-seed flavor that you can almost visualize a barefoot Sy romping through a dream-like childhood.

- John Loom had an opposite upbringing. A native of a large Eastern city, John's personality is very polished . . . his parents were not only rich but also part of "high society." Result: John is sophisticated in manners and conversation. Yet, he tempers this polish with an easy wit, a smile that forms quickly and a down-to-earth naturalness. His total personality is quite pleasing and enjoyable.

- Although Joe O'Brien also owns a winning smile and a quick, easy wit, he uses them very differently. As opposed to John's sophistication, Joe reflects his Irish heritage. His wit is more of the banter type . . . at the snap of a finger he is ready to tell a joke or engage in a good-natured argument. Yet the difference is only one of style and not one of effect, for both John and Joe can liven up a conversation.

- On the other hand, Tom Trench is an enthusiastic, hard-driving businessman. You know the type . . . a fast mind tied to a cautious tongue. Ideas and thoughts form quickly in his mind, yet he will consider them carefully before he speaks them aloud. But when he does talk his voice almost throbs with the dynamic enthusiasm that is such a natural part of his personality.

Sy, John, Joe, Tom . . . each has a personality that is colorful enough to add life and excitement to a conversation. In essence their personalities each become a specialist's reservoir.

Perhaps your personality can be used in this way, too. To discover if it can, go back to the question you asked yourself when reading these case histories . . . "Why is this fellow's personality appealing?"

The answer: each fellow has a personality that is completely natural . . . none of them forces himself or acts out a role. If you are blessed with a personality that is truly outgoing, pleasing and captivating, then you, too, can safely use it as part of your specialist's reservoir . . . it will add life and excitement to your conversations.

HOW TO CULTIVATE YOUR OWN INTERESTS

Earlier we discussed building part of your knowledge reservoir around the interest of your acquaintances. Now let's see how to use your own interests as a rich source of material that will add sparkle to your conversations.

Start by asking yourself: "What do I find interesting?" The best way to answer this question is by approaching it in a workmanlike manner . . . take a pencil and paper, and then reflect over the past few months.

Think about your conversations . . .

. . . were any of your conversations interesting enough to get you excited and enthusiastic? Write down the topics of these conversations.

Recall what you read . . .

. . . did you find any newspaper or magazine articles so interesting that you automatically picked up a pencil and underlined the key thoughts? Did any articles so intrigue you that you re-read them again just to be sure you didn't miss any important points? Did any articles so capture your imagination that you discussed them with someone else? Write down the topics of these articles.

Remember TV shows and movies . . .

. . . did you see any that caught your interest more

strongly than the average show? Analyze the ones that come to mind . . . what was the show or movie about? Write its topic down on the paper also.

By now the average person should have at least twelve topics listed . . . if you've done a really thorough job of searching your memory, you'll have listed many more than a dozen.

Then condense the list . . .

. . . by combining the different topics where you can and eliminating the less interesting topics one by one until you have only three left. These three should be the ones that arouse the greatest enthusiasm in your mind. These are the topics where your interest is so strong that you will enjoy every minute you spend gathering the knowledge you'll need to stock a specialist's reservoir. And because each topic is plugged directly into your interests, you will surely talk about it with enthusiasm. Here are some examples of how other conversationalists have put such a specialist's reservoir to good use:

- Mary O'Neil enjoys cooking so much that she owns a library of cookbooks running the gamut from fancy French cooking to outdoor hamburger grilling. Result: Mary's knowledge reservoir runs so deep that she can hold another woman's interest for hours . . . she's able to discuss almost any recipe you name, and she also knows the history of how these dishes came to be created. Further, she's eager to share her knowledge by giving hints on how to make meals more flavorful. I can remember her once telling some other women, "Did you know that the water you use for cooking is important? Soft water is the best. I first suspected this when I took a tour of a coffee processor's plant. At the end of the tour he gave us the best coffee I ever tasted. Although I've tried his brand, I've never been able to capture the same taste. I'm positive that the difference between his coffee and mine is the kind of water he used."
- Fred Moran loves sports . . . he knows the batting average of every player in both baseball leagues, plus

their runs batted in, bases stolen, and even the weight of the bat they use. When baseball season passes, it's football time, then basketball and hockey, then spring training time again. Fred is never at a loss for words the year around; he can even quote statistics from the Olympics: "Did you know that the United States has won 15 out of the last 17 shot put competitions? And the record throw is over 67 feet. That's almost double the under 37 feet that won back in 1896!"

• Sam Perrone loves another type of competition—politics. He's read all the local library books on this topic and keeps up-to-date on current happenings as well. Consequently, he's an expert on the "ins" and "outs" of political thinking and maneuvering; he also can tell you all about the habits and techniques of each major politician. Whenever there's a discussion of current political events, you can count on Sam to add some background color:

You: "Wasn't that a great speech Mayor Frederick made last night?"

Sam: "Sure was. And it won't hurt his re-election chances either. His stand on school budgets is right in line with the way many people are thinking . . ."

You can easily become as knowledgeable as Mary, Fred or Sam simply by working with the list of interests you compiled earlier. Start with the topic that excites you the most, and learn all you can about it. Then having mastered topic one, go on to the second. Finally, conquer the third. When researching topics that hold such personal interest, you'll find time passing so quickly and effortlessly that you'll enjoy every moment of it.

And by developing both a generalist's and a specialist's reservoir, you will have the knowledge you need for almost any conversational situation. You'll be able to speak on a wide range of topics while also possessing a depth of knowledge in specific areas.

8

Tested Ways to Add Exciting Dimensions to Your Conversation

Sought-after conversationalists never stop learning . . . you learn to do your job better . . . you learn to stretch your money further . . . you learn to play golf or bridge better . . . and you also learn to converse better. Yes, you add excitement to your life and conversation because you never stop learning no matter how old you are. And that is good!

You can make it even better by using the same learning techniques that helped you in your school days. True, you no longer have trained teachers to help you; but this isn't a loss, it's a great opportunity . . . you now can take the initiative to decide for yourself what you want to learn . . . you can choose the most convenient time to study . . . you are in the driver's seat. You can teach yourself what *you* think is best to learn, and you can schedule this learning for times best for you. Luckily, there are many sources where you can turn for self-teaching help.

In the preceding chapter, you started building the kind of knowledge reservoir that will assure exciting conversations. And by now, much of what you learned has become an instinctive part of you and has added to your conversational abilities.

In this chapter you'll learn the tested and easy-to-use techniques that successful conversationalists use to keep their knowledge reservoir continually growing.

THIS KEY UNLOCKS THE WORLD'S STOREHOUSE OF KNOWLEDGE

Sooner or later all the world's knowledge ends up on a printed page. You're well aware of this each time you catch up on current events by reading a daily newspaper or a weekly magazine. A few quick moments spent reading and you're automatically holding your own in any conversation on current events.

And it'll pay off if you go a step further and read some history books. Too many people think history books are dry . . . they couldn't be more mistaken. History isn't dead . . . it's the fascinating summary of the current events of many yesterdays. It's also a quick and easy way to gain insight into your world. Every good conversationalist I know has a sense of history . . . I don't mean that he's memorized a list of dates and places, but that he has a talking knowledge of important people, cultures and events of the past. Though it's rare for an event to repeat itself exactly as it occurred in the past, the same basic principles influence what happens in century after century. Once you take a few minutes to gain an understanding of these basic principles they will stay with you all your life. This pays off by helping you better understand the meaning of what's going on today and by adding to your ability to speak meaningfully about current events.

Outstanding conversationalists seek more than just a sense of history when they read. You can, too. Read top-notch novels . . . they will give you excellent insights into human nature. Read reference books . . . they will help develop the generalist's reservoirs discussed in the previous chapter. Yes, reading unlocks the world's storehouse of knowledge.

AN EASY METHOD THAT SPEEDS YOUR LEARNING

Obviously you cannot read your way through a library, so here's an easy system that will help you choose the reference books that best build your knowledge reservoir.

First, glance through the card files in your local library. Note what books are available in those topic areas where you decided to broaden your knowledge.

Second, go to the proper shelves and glance through the books themselves, using the Easy Review Method described on this page. Make a list of which books present the information you want to learn. Then, number the listed books in the order they should be read, starting with the simpler ones and progressing toward the more advanced.

Third, take the lowest numbered book with you as you leave the library. After you have digested its contents, read the other numbered books until all of them have been mentally absorbed and the knowledge within them safely stored in your mental reservoir.

Fourth, as you are picking up new knowledge, start putting it to conversational use right away. This immediate use reinforces your reading and helps you remember the new facts. It also adds to your knowledge reservoir ... as you know, talking to other people is a great way to learn.

So far, so good ... you're building the knowledge that makes you the equal of any conversationalist. And you can learn almost as well by yourself as you would under a teacher's guidance by using the Easy Review Method. Many experts have worked hard on finding ways to speed up "book learning" while increasing the amount of knowledge gathered. This Easy Review Method summarizes their findings:

- *Preview the book ...*

    ... Read the contents slowly, then read the author's preface or introduction. These will give you an idea of what the book has to say.

- *Preview each chapter ...*

    ... Before you begin reading each chapter, read the opening paragraphs, then read the first sentence of each following paragraph. If there are subheads, as there are in this book, read the first and last paragraph under each subhead. Finally read the closing paragraphs, then state to yourself the chapter's main ideas in a few simple sentences.

- *Read the chapter ...*

    ... After you're familiar with the major ideas in the chapter, you'll find that you can read fairly fast. For example, don't read individual words ... read a phrase or a thought unit of words. And don't be afraid you'll miss something; by reading fast you force yourself to concentrate on your reading.

- *Write an outline ...*

    ... Immediately after reading each chapter, write a

short but complete outline listing the main thoughts
of that chapter.

• *Review each chapter* . . .
. . . After you're finished reading the book, review it
chapter by chapter. Start by reading your outline
summary of the chapter and then skim through that
chapter's pages noting its main ideas.

Obviously, these techniques work best with non-fiction
books. There is a technique, however, that works well with
fiction . . . that is underlining key ideas or placing a check mark
next to them in the margin. A quick review of these pencil
marks after the novel is finished can help to implant these key
thoughts in your mind.

This technique is a real winner. As George Reade once told
me, "If I didn't use the Easy Review Method, I'd never have
been able to build the wide-ranging reservoir that has been so
helpful to me in conversations."

TAKING HOLD OF THE WORD TOOLS YOU NEED

When you have the right tools, any job is easier . . . preparing firewood is much simpler if you have a sharp bow saw
to cut your logs and two heavy wedges plus a sledge hammer to
split them. The same is true for conversation . . . try explaining
something without using the proper word tools and it's sheer
frustration. For example, sixth-grade students would be confused if their teacher said, "Pretend you are going to a
symposium and write a paper outlining what we've recently
studied about weather."

I doubt if any sixth-grader knows that a symposium is a
technical meeting where several speakers deliver short papers on
related topics. The teacher would have been wiser to say, "Write
a report you can read to the class on what you have learned
about weather."

The best way to build the inventory of words you'll need
is by owning an up-to-date dictionary and working with it in the
same way that conversationalists like George Reade do:

Put time into your look-up . . .
. . . After you look up the meaning or spelling of a

word, stop before you shut the pages and glance at a few extra words. Set a goal for yourself: whenever you look up a word, study at least three other words at the same time. Set another goal: consult your dictionary at least once a day, even if you just open it and read about the first three words you see.

Put meaning into your look-up . . .

. . . Very few words have only one meaning, so when you look up a word, think carefully about its different shades of meaning and you'll be able to use the word much more effectively in your conversation. For example, think about the word "obey." Does it mean "to comply with an order" or "to follow guidance?" According to Webster both are correct. Yet, how many people you know would use the word "obey" in its second meaning? Try an intriguing experiment by asking a number of your friends these two questions:

    (1) "How would you react if your boss ordered you to help a fellow worker?"

    (2) "How would you react if your boss offered you some guidance on how to do your job?"

Chances are most people would answer the first question, "I would *obey* his order." And they would answer the second question, "I would *accept* his advice. Knowing this you would only use the word "obey" in its first meaning. This would build a reputation for you as a good user of words.

Put effort into your look-up . . .

. . . In the definition of the word "obey," my edition of Webster capitalizes the word "execute." Out of interest I turned to "execute" and found five different definitions. Right now, without opening your dictionary, can you give five different definitions to the word "execute?" If not, make the effort to look them up, you'll find the information will enrich your conversation.

Immediately under these five definitions my dictionary gives a six-line paragraph describing the fine shadings of difference between the two synonyms: "execute" and "administer." Off the top of your head, can you describe the difference between these two words? If not, make the effort to look them up.

The point is clear . . . it's so much easier to perform as a conversationalist when you have the proper word tools. And the simple way to stock up on these tools is to use your dictionary every day . . . and to invest time, meaning, and effort each time you use it.

QUESTIONS THAT ENRICH
WHAT YOUR SENSES GRASP

The raw material you need to broaden your conversation is all around you. And you'll note its presence much more easily when you follow these three techniques:

- Alert your senses to your surroundings.
  (By now you've had some time to work with the waking-up techniques you learned in the last chapter. This new skill will serve you well as you move on toward improving your conversational abilities.)
- Absorb what your newly-awakened senses note.
- Think about what you have absorbed.

Once your senses are fully opened, you can easily assure that they'll broaden your conversation by asking yourself questions such as:

"How alert am I to noticing beauty so I can use it to enrich my conversation?" The next time you go outside look closely at the flowers growing in your yard . . . observe their soft petals and subtle blending of colors. Look up at a tree . . . don't just glance quickly, but relax and really see the tree . . . count how many shades of green leaves you see growing on the intertwined branches. Then while you are quiet and relaxed, and your senses are open, stand still and

listen . . . really hear the birds, let their songs be more than only a background noise. Yes, the beauty of nature is yours for the enjoying and conversing . . . all you need to do is open up your senses.

Man also creates beauty . . . in music, pictures, words, dance . . . in many forms. Ballet, for example, combines music and dance. Now I'll admit that not everyone likes ballet. But even if you don't like it, go to one sometime as Fred Watson did. As Fred sat there he kept asking himself, "What does this mean? What are the music and the dancer's motion trying to tell me?" Later he confessed to me that, "I'm still not a fan of ballet, but I certainly was surprised how well the dancers and music worked together. They really conveyed a message to me without using words." Try a similar experiment . . . I'm sure you'll also be amazed at how well man-made beauty can communicate a meaning, and how this meaning can be the base for an interesting conversation.

"Do I take advantage of the knowledge owned by other people?" Go out of your way to talk with other people . . . go beyond pleasantries in your conversations and discuss subjects where other people have strong knowledge and interests. These are excellent ways to get to know other people and to broaden yourself at the same time. In fact, it's so good that it's worth your while actually to create opportunities for discussion rather than just waiting for them to come along accidentally. There are many ways to create these opportunities. For example, join the PTA and seek out areas where you can help the school improve its ability to educate. Or become active in your church or in community service groups. Scott Trion did this and soon gained a reputation as an outgoing and alert person. Others with this type of personality sought his friendship. It wasn't long before Scott was associating with active people who had active minds. These new friendships increased his knowledge reservoir and added sparkle and breadth to his conversation.

"Do I learn from plays and TV performances?" Make it a habit to watch public affairs and drama shows on TV, and also to attend plays periodically put on by local theater groups. When watching a TV drama or theater play, ask yourself questions as the plot unfolds, "Why was that line funny? How

did the actor help the humor come across?"

Do the same for other emotions. "How did the actor's voice inflection and body movement help communicate his anger? How did I know the actor was frustrated even though he didn't say he was?" It is amazing how much you can learn simply by observing.

Eric Lyon always goes to the theater with friends who are good at expressing their thoughts and feelings. Then during intermission and driving home, Eric discusses the play with them. He asks them what message they got from the play . . . how it meshed with their own experiences . . . what parts of the play they found most meaningful.

The best way to approach these topics in conversations is first by expressing your own feelings, then asking your friends for their opinions: "Remember when Floyd and his father were arguing, how they both saw only their own point of view and paid no attention to the other's? Didn't that strike you the same way it did me? It reminded me of many arguments I've been in."

"Do I hold armchair debates?" Here's another way to profit from theater and TV presentations: first, view them with other people; then spark a debate about the more controversial parts of the show. It doesn't really matter what viewpoint you take in the debate; the exchange of ideas that occurs helps you gain new insights into the issues being discussed and thereby adds breadth to your conversation.

SECRETS THAT MAKE EVEN LOCAL
TRAVEL STIMULATING

"Get out into this world," was once an advertising slogan for an airline, and it isn't a bad one for a conversationalist as well. Travel adds breadth to your conversation by stretching your mind:

It exposes you to new experiences. . . .
. . . At home you'll respond automatically to familiar surroundings, but in a new locality you are forced to stop and think before you respond. For example, when you buy a shirt in the United States you glance

at the price tag, pull out your wallet and pay for it . . . you know exactly what it costs. But travel into Canada and the dollar's value changes. Before you know how much a shirt will cost, you must ask yourself two questions: "How much does this shirt cost in Canadian money? What's this equal to in American money?"

It exposes you to new people. . . .

. . . When conversing with people you know you again can react automatically, but when talking with new people, you must first evaluate each new personality before you speak . . . you must decide how to express yourself so that you'll be understood. To continue the previous illustration, if you travel to northeastern Canada, you'll come to Quebec, where French is the major language. Not everyone speaks English, and those who do often don't speak it well. I can recall conversing with two college students from Montreal. First I asked, "What are you majoring in?" Blank faces stared back at me. Then I said, "What courses are taking?" More blank looks. Finally, "What are you studying?" Then I received a smile, a nod, and an answer. An hour later when the conversation ended, my mind really had been stretched, for I had to rephrase each statement two or three times before it was understood.

FINDING VITAL EXPERIENCES
WHEREVER YOU GO

Perhaps the most voiced objection to travel is, "It's too expensive." True, it costs money to travel out of the country or to cross the United States. But the kind of travel that stretches your mind shouldn't be measured in miles; it should be measured in the amount of exposure you have to new people, new ideas, new places, new experiences.

I can remember George Reade telling me, "When I travel across the street to a neighbor's house I'm exposed to someone who has a different life style, a different value structure and a different sense of priorities. And when I travel from my home, I can find someone who's so completely different from me that exposure to him stretches my mind as much as if I had traveled to the other end of the country and met someone new."

What George says rings true. For example, I once lived near a couple where the husband had given up his own business and had taken a job as a laborer. His wife got a job to compensate for the lower income. Result: they have more time in the evenings and weekends for each other. How different this life style is from another neighbor's, Norm Lasker, who spends five days a week traveling in his sales job and hardly sees his family.

How do you find people with such differing viewpoints? Simple. Just be friendly. Talk to your nearby neighbors. Take evening walks and speak to people you pass by. Don't rush from PTA or other community meetings . . . take a few minutes to get to know the others present. You'll find this time well invested . . . it'll help broaden both your outlook and your conversation.

Yes, you can gain all the conversational values of mind-stretching encounters right in your own community. The key to whether or not you gain these values lies in how you pick your conversational partners. It's only human to associate with people who think and act as you do, but this doesn't stretch your mind. If you wish to add breadth to your conversation, also talk to people who don't act or think as you do. And there are many such people living within a few minutes of your home. All you have to do is seek them out.

Travel is more than just meeting someone new; it's also exposing yourself to new ideas and ways of living that differ from your own. Again, you don't have to travel far. One technique that Lyle Redt uses is to visit a local museum . . . it's a rich source of information about the world of nature and about the way people lived in the past. As Lyle explained to me, "Let's face it, the past isn't dead . . . it's simply the early chapters in the ongoing story of life. Thus, studying the past helps me stretch my mind and helps me converse in the present."

There's bound to be a museum in your area or in a nearby city. Travel to it at least twice a year. The museum doesn't have to be big and fancy; even if it covers only local history, it can still add breadth to your knowledge and sparkle to your conversation.

While museums expose you to yesterday's life, your local community exposes you to the "here and now." For example, here is a seasonal list of some of the mind-stretchers I enjoy in my community:

Fall. In addition to the traditional sports and political activities, there is one outstanding cultural event. Paintings, sculptures and many other types of art are exhibited in a local park. This annual event is so well known that people come from miles around to display their work or to browse.

Winter. Local high school auditoriums throughout the township play weekend host to symphonies, dramas, comedies and individual concert performances. This is also the time when social action groups present lectures, demonstrations and other programs to dramatize their causes.

Spring. This is the perfect time to visit the local parks and planting fields where much can be learned and enjoyed as different plants and flowers respond to the warming weather.

Summer. Outdoor concerts and theaters-in-the-round are just two of the many conversation-enriching events offered during July and August.

True, not all communities have such a variety of cultural opportunities, but every town has some form of performing art or community event nearby. Travel to it and reap the conversation-broadening benefits that it offers.

MAKING YOUR WEEKENDS CONVERSATIONAL TREASURIES

Take a map of your locality . . . measure the distance you can drive in an hour . . . then using this as a radius, draw a circle around the town where you live.

Now draw two more circles: one for two hours and one for four hours drive from your home. Draw a final circle for a seven hours drive.

Next locate all places worth visiting that lie within the circled areas. For example, note museums and formal gardens . . . theaters ... historical locations such as Teddy Roosevelt's home or Abe Lincoln's birthplace . . . national parks that offer conducted tours or that have talks on the park's outstanding features. In other words, any place you can visit that will add breadth to your conversational reservoir should be listed.

How do you discover all these interesting locations? Some of them will be shown right on your map while others will require a little searching on your part. Here are four techniques that I've often used to uncover places worth visiting:

- Ask your friends. Every friend you speak to should know at least one place worth seeing.
- Write the Department of Parks in your state capital and in nearby states asking them for a listing of parks, historical locations and recreational sites within the state.
- Send another letter to the Department of Conservation in your state capital and in nearby states requesting a list of all areas under their jurisdiction which are open to the public. In most states, the information you get from the Park and Conservation Departments will not be the same.
- Call the libraries, civic associations and town halls in the cities and towns that lie within the circled areas. They can often tell you of local places worth visiting; if not they can refer you to someone who can.

After you have asked, written and phoned, note on your map all the locations you have discovered. Then set up a travel schedule that will boost the conversational abilities of your family. Here's the way Mat Reilly and his wife schedule their time:

- Every four to six weeks they visit a location within the one- and two-hour circles. They travel one hour's drive one time and two hour's drive the next. This mixing is particularly helpful since the Reillys have youngsters—children will quickly lose interest in traveling if you take too many trips where they have to sit in the car for two hours, visit a location, then sit for a two-hour return trip home.

- Four times a year they travel to a location within the four-hour circle. They make these weekend trips and stay overnight at their destination.

- On three-day weekends, they head off to a spot located out in the seven-hour circle. Leaving at six o'clock in the morning, the Reillys are there by 3:00 PM ... in plenty of time to settle in and become somewhat familiar with the area. The whole second day is theirs to enjoy. Leaving about 3:00 PM on the third day, the Reillys are home in time to get a good night's sleep before returning to work. This schedule will expose you to the broadening influence of a new environment for the equivalent of two full days.

Taking all that your world can give you

If weekends can take you so far afield, just imagine how far you can go on a two week vacation ... if you travel by plane, you can spend over a week and a half in any place in the world. What a knowledge reservoir boosting experience that can be!

The way to get the greatest conversation-broadening value from your vacation is to pick your spot, travel there, then relax and enjoy your visit the way we do by using the Rule of the Three P's:

- *Present*

  Don't just limit yourself to visiting the tourist attractions ... expose yourself to the area's everyday life as well by joining in the community activities. For example, when last in Maine I attended the Sunday services of a small local church. The way the minister preached his sermon opened my eyes to how closely the "Downeaster" is tied to the sea. For many years after that visit I have been able to use this information when conversing with people who were planning trips to the state of Maine.

- *Past*

Museums, libraries and the local people are the three main sources you can use to learn about the history of the area where you are staying. Look for two types of information:

Learn about the distant past. Knowledge of the early history of an area is a rich source of conversational material when you later tell your friends about your vacation. For example, when camping at the Samuel deChamplain Provincial Park, I asked one of my Canadian hosts how the park got its name. I was told, "It's named after the famous explorer and looks the same now as it did over 300 years ago when Champlain explored this part of Canada by canoeing down the Mattawa River."

Become familiar with the more recent past. Your visit will take on much more meaning when you have a feel for how the local townspeople live. For example, I learned something about the hard life of small farmers in Montana when I talked to a clerk in a local store. "I once had a cattle ranch far from town," he told me. "It was hard living but we were getting by. Then they cancelled the school bus and told me my son had to spend winters in town so he could get his schooling. Since I couldn't afford to pay his room and board plus run the ranch, I had to sell out, move into town and take a job in this store. During the summer we make extra money by working a small wheat farm from daybreak to noon. Then we come back into town and I work at the store until 9:00 PM. It's tough, but at least my boy is getting an education." As you can imagine, I've often used this story to add interest to conversations.

- *People*

As in the Montana example, don't just buy from the

local tradespeople, talk to them as well. Learn how
they feel about their way of life, about their
locality, about current issues and events. Note how
they talk and the values on which they base their
opinions. Then, when later discussing your vacation
with your friends, you'll be able to hold them
spellbound with your insights into different areas of
the country.

Yes, whether you go across the street or across the sea,
travel adds breadth and sparkle to your conversation. By
exposing yourself to new places and new people, you can
stretch your mind and deepen your perspective. You don't have
to travel far . . . the only requirement is that you travel with an
open mind. Do so and you'll surely be a sought-after conversationalist.

9

Taking Command of a Group Conversation

Often a conversation rolls forward as smoothly as a well-trained football team moves downfield for a touchdown. When you see this kind of conversation underway, you know it isn't happening by accident; you can bet that someone is gently, yet firmly guiding it in a forward direction.

A football team consists of eleven men, each a professional capable of doing his job on his own. But the team can't win unless it works together as a unit, following the instructions of its leader ... the quarterback. He knows what his teammates can do best and calls the plays that make good use of these strengths.

This same principle holds true for conversation. Here, too, each person can be able to converse well; but unless someone calls the plays the conversation will not start moving forward smoothly, and the people in the group will not really enjoy themselves.

Because of the conversational skills you've mastered as you have been reading this book, you should "quarterback" the conversation, gently guiding it in a forward moving direction. These skills make you uniquely qualified to take on the job. And it's not a hard job either ... to get a group conversation started, all you have to do is follow the few simple principles given in this chapter.

HOW TO BLEND MANY
PERSONALITIES TOGETHER

"When I'm starting a conversation," George Reade once told me, "I always try to make sure that everyone present enjoys himself right from the beginning." He went on to explain that "one good way of doing this is by noting the personalities of each person present ... then guiding the discussion so that these personalities don't clash with each other. In fact, if possible I try to blend the personalities together in a friendly way." George's technique is a good one . . . I've also used it when quarterbacking conversations. For example, when starting a conversation with Charles and Larry, I first determine the basic personality type of each man. If Charles is very outgoing and aggressive, while Larry is quiet and sensitive . . . then I do try to keep the discussion centered on topics where they both hold the same opinion. This way Charles doesn't force his viewpoints on Larry, and Larry doesn't sulk away from the conversation with hurt feelings. Result: Both Larry and Charles enjoy themselves and I gain an even stronger reputation as an astute conversationalist.

As the above example shows, you don't have to dig deeply into each personality . . . in fact, you can easily define someone's personality by using the general categories you're now familiar with from the earlier chapter, entitled "Short Cuts For Instantly Deciding How To Converse With Any Stranger." As a refresher, here are some questions based on these short cuts that fit people into general personality groups:

- Can he be easily drawn into a discussion or is he afraid to speak for fear he may make a mistake? Is he quiet? Is he outgoing and, if so, does he use his enthusiasm in a natural and healthy way, or does he try to dominate the conversation?

- Does he use ten-dollar words, or everyday language? Does he think in a theoretical, blue-sky way, or does his mind work in a more practical and earthy way?

- Is he an aggressive type who likes to out-talk other people . . . or is he sensitive, easily offended and possibly lacking in self confidence?

- Is he a pie-in-the-sky idealist or a feet-on-the-ground realist?

- How strong is his ego . . . does it require special handling, or is it of average strength?

- Is he usually positive or negative in the way he thinks?

Use these questions when starting a conversation as I did in the previous Charley and Larry example. The questions make it easy to gain a rough idea of the personalities of your conversation partners. In the example they prevented Charley's opinionated viewpoints from offending Larry's sensitivities. In other conversations you can reword intellectually-phrased remarks so that they're clearly understood by down-to-earth talkers ... or you can prevent hard-headed realists from exchanging angry words with strong-willed idealists ... or you can handle someone's ego needs in a way that doesn't interfere with the flow of conversation between the less egotistic people in a discussion.

All you need is a rough idea of the personality of the other people present in order to start a good conversation. These questions give you this knowledge in a simple way ... they give you the know-how you need to guide the discussion gently so that the personalities blend together and do not clash ... this will leave everyone feeling that the conversation was both interesting and enjoyable for him personally, and that you did an excellent job of starting and guiding the discussion.

"Boy, was I ever bored talking to those deadheads."
"That conversation certainly was a waste of time."

Have you ever said words like these after leaving a discussion? I sure have. Why did I feel that way? Because no one made me feel that I was an important part of the conversation.

The only way I, or anyone else for that matter, really enjoy a conversation is when I become personally involved in the topics being discussed. And this is only natural ... a pleasant, pass-the-time-of-day conversation is okay ... but it isn't very exciting. Surely it helps the minutes pass without too much aggravation, but it's like watching someone else eat a two-inch thick steak ... there is no personal satisfaction.

That's why I always use the following two techniques when quarterbacking a conversation ... they're designed to help make the other people feel important, to make them feel involved.

CHOOSING TOPICS THAT STIMULATE
OTHERS IN THE GROUP

When you are noting the personalities of the other people in order to blend them together, try to uncover some of their interests at the same time. Here are two ways I've found helpful:

Use your ears... people usually talk about subjects on which they've built a knowledge reservoir; after all, these are the topics on which they can speak most confidently. So open your ears and note who is the first person to introduce a new topic into the conversation ... if Burt is the first to speak up about last night's basketball game, you can bet that this is a topic that interests him. While your ears are open listen for the sound of enthusiasm ... if Sara talks more enthusiastically when flowers are discussed, you know that this topic interests her ... excitement in a person's voice is a good clue that the topic being discussed stimulates his interest.

Use your eyes... many people communicate how they feel about something by the way they move their body ... they try to physically move away from topics where they feel uncomfortable and move toward subjects that interest them:

- Red O'Leary always leans forward in his chair when a topic interests him; he seems to push back against the chair when a topic makes him feel uncomfortable.
- Bob Lord clenches and grinds his teeth when he doesn't like a topic, while Wally Porter tenses his arm muscles. Both Bob and Wally relax when the topic is more to their liking.
- Tom Blandamere uses his arms expressively. When he feels threatened by a topic, he crosses them, and you intuitively feel he's on the defensive. Change the topic to one that interests him, and his arms fall to his side, he opens up and he talks in a relaxed manner.

So make a mental note whenever you see someone physically react to a topic under discussion. It's easy enough to do.

After you have watched a person react to several different topics, you will begin to get a feel for his interests.

Once you're familiar with the interests of each person in a group you can combine these interests into categories and seek a common denominator.

For example, what would you say is a common denominator for the interests of Sally Roll, Joe Wallach and Jim Arons. Sally is interested in square dancing, Joe sings in choral groups and Jim coaches a teen-age basketball team. You are right if you say that a common factor is a basic interest in doing things with other people. So in a conversation with Sally, Joe and Jim, discuss topics that involve group activities and you'll have a better than average chance of capturing the interest of these three people and starting an enthusiastic conversation.

When the group is fairly large and you can't find a common interest denominator, compromise by first discussing a topic that interests most of the people, and as the conversation progresses bring up topics that appeal to the others. This way everyone will have enjoyed talking about at least one topic that interests him.

PREVENTING OTHERS FROM SHIFTING THEIR MENTAL GEARS INTO NEUTRAL

When you start a conversation by choosing topics that interest the other people present, you'll want to handle these topics in a way that involves these other people mentally. If you are with strong baseball fans, for example, guide the conversation away from statistics such as runs batted in and bases stolen . . . the only mental effort these require is the ability to remember numbers. Rather ask questions that make the others think: "Which pitchers do you think the Mets should use to beat the Dodgers in their upcoming three-game series?" Or, "How do you think the Yankees could be made stronger by trading players with other teams?"

By asking questions that make other people put on their thinking caps, you force them to become involved in the topic they're discussing. They'll enjoy the conversation more, and they'll think more highly of your ability to quarterback a conversation. When they feel like having an interesting discussion, they'll automatically want you to join them.

Asking questions is an easy technique to use. The others are doing the work ... they're thinking up the answers. You don't have to offer judgments or opinions on their answers ... just listen carefully enough to their opinions to catch an idea or two for more questions to ask.

INTRODUCING QUESTIONS THAT
WAKE EVERYONE UP

Although asking questions is a simple technique, it involves others personally in the conversation because it forces them to come to grips mentally with both the topic and the other people. A discussion on the local school system, for example, could easily become a boring listing of what people don't like about the schools. If this happens, the conversation serves no purpose other than to let some people vent their emotions, and it certainly doesn't help build your reputation as an accomplished conversationalist. When discussing a topic such as the local schools, it's much better to involve the participants mentally by asking questions such as:

> **"What do you think the school board should do to improve the quality of the education provided by our schools?"**
> **"How can we convince the school board to act on our ideas?"**

If the group strongly disagrees with the way the schools are run, then maybe they would enjoy discussing how to elect a new school board member who agrees with their opinions. This would lead to conversation-starting questions such as:

- **"What major issues should he base his platform on?"**
- **"What position should he take on these issues?"**
- **"Would this platform attract enough voters to get him elected?"**

Other questions you could use as conversation starters are:

- **"How good a job is being done by the grade school**

principal?" "By the high school principal?" "By the superintendent of schools?"

- "In general, how good are the teachers in the system? How well do they know the subjects they teach?" "How dedicated are they to helping the children learn?"
- "Do they do a good job of motivating the kids, of making the children want to learn?"
- "Do they keep the parents advised of problems the children are having with their school work?" "Do they work with the parents in trying to help the kids correct their problems?"

These are just a few of the many questions that could be raised . . . all aimed at the general idea: How can we improve the quality of our local schools?

Conversations like this never let people shift their mental gears into neutral because they force people to think. And as people start to think, they become mentally involved; they grow a bit. Through interaction with others their opinions become modified and refined, so that when the conversation ends they know a little more than they did before it began . . . they leave the conversation with that feeling of satisfaction that comes from learning something new. And since you're the person who quarterbacked the conversation, you're the hero in their minds . . . you're the one who made the conversation so exciting.

LAUNCHING A CONVERSATIONAL
CHAIN REACTION

Once you've got a conversation started, you want to make sure it doesn't die after the first comment or two. And as before, involving the others in the conversation is the key. Get them involved and the conversation will grow as each person contributes his own thoughts and opinions on the topic. Soon the discussion starts to take on a personality of its own and starts to generate its own forward momentum. As it does, your quarterbacking job becomes easier and easier.

A simple way to assure that the others become involved is

to plan ahead of time what you want the discussion to cover. In the school conversation you could follow this general outline:

- Ask the others what they think the problems are in their school district.
- Help them to define what they think caused these problems.
- Encourage them to come up with possible solutions to these problems.

An outline is a handy tool. In the words of George Reade, "I always find an outline invaluable. It helps me guide the discussion forward from one logical step to the next." George is right; an outline can be an invaluable tool. For example, if you were to work with the school outline, here's how it could help you quarterback the conversation.

Draw out the problems.

Although you are asking the other people for their opinions in this step, you want them to do more than just to say the first thing that pops into their minds; you want them to dig into the subject and really think about it. If Sandra Talley says, "Johnny doesn't get good marks in math," she is making such a general remark that it doesn't add much to the conversation. But it is a good starting point from which you can draw out a specific problem. So you would quarterback the conversation by asking Sally questions until you find out that, "Johnny knows his math facts, but he doesn't understand how to apply them when solving problems." Now the conversation has uncovered two important points.

- Johnny Talley has been taught the basic math facts, so there's no problem here.
- The problem is that he hasn't learned how to apply the facts he's been taught.

Define the causes of each problem.

Now that you have uncovered a problem you have a perfect opportunity to start the others contributing to the topic . . . you can guide their thinking gently by getting them to dig into the problem and find out what caused it. The easiest way to do this is to use thought-starting questions like these:

- "Many of our children have also had problems with math. Do you think that our teachers are not communicating well? How good a job do you think our teachers are doing in showing our children how to use math facts?"
- And if it turns out that the teachers are communicating well, then you could see if there is a time problem . . . you could ask, "Does the teacher spend enough class time working on math problems?"

Finally, if you learned that the teacher is doing a good job, then you might suspect that the problem lies in Johnny Talley and not the teacher. Let's be honest, not every child wants to learn . . . many prefer to spend time in fun and games. Joan Randolf found this out about her son not too long ago. She was quarterbacking a conversation much like the one we've been discussing here. As she asked questions about other children she slowly started to realize that her own son wasn't trying as hard as he could. Result: After cooperative effort with her son's teacher, Joan's son is now doing much better.

When defining the cause of the problem, everyone is still digging into the problem as they did in the first step. But now they are digging more deeply, their thinking is more intense; each person is putting forth greater effort and therefore getting back greater pleasure from the conversation . . . and the more they dig on their own, the easier it becomes for you to quarterback.

Encourage people to come up with solutions.

Once everyone agrees on the problem's cause, your next step is so simple that it's automatic . . . start discussing how to eliminate the cause. In this third step, the people grow a little more . . . they go further than analyzing a problem . . . they think creatively and search for solutions. When people reach this stage, their involvement in the conversation is complete. You have succeeded in starting a group conversation that holds everyone's interest.

10

How to Keep a Group Conversation Enthusiastic

In Chapter 9 you learned how to apply many of the conversational skills you've mastered so far ... and you've learned how to use them to take command of a group conversation. Now let's see how these same skills can be used to keep the newly-created conversation moving in a forward direction. This is mostly a job of preventing the wrong things from happening. I can remember one dark night in Maine when Steve Kern and I were returning by boat from an island to the mainland. Steve asked me to sit up in the front bow of the boat with a flashlight and warn him if we came too near any buoys that marked submerged lobster pots. Keeping a group conversation moving forward is much like this ... you'll sit up front and look out for anything that might harm the conversation.

HOLDING THE TEMPERATURE AT A PRODUCTIVE LEVEL

As people's involvement in a conversation increases, it becomes more and more difficult for them to keep an open mind ... their emotions start to creep into their thinking and then into their conversation. So at this point start paying attention to the temperature level of the participants; you don't want anyone to get hot under the collar and wreck a conversation with the white-hot heat of his temper. Here's some of the more common temperature-raisers.

The emotional complaint. This is usually a very general statement and thus can be easily handled by forcing the complainer to become more specific. Here's how Joan Randolf did this when quarterbacking the school conversation discussed in the last chapter:

If someone said:	*Then she restored objectivity by asking:*
"That teacher is just no good."	"Why isn't the teacher any good?" After the person answered, Joan then asked, "How can she improve?"
"That school policy is rotten."	"What is wrong with the policy?" After the person answered, Joan asked, "What should it be?"

Joan's technique is worth taking a closer look at. First, she responds to a general emotional complaint with a question designed to force the speaker to be more specific. Then Joan asks the speaker for a possible solution. These two types of questions automatically force the speaker's thinking to become objective and logical; they cool the speaker down before he has a chance to inject an emotional atmosphere into the conversation.

Strong and clashing opinions. John O'Keefe might suggest: "Our major problem is lack of space; we need to build a new school."

Jack Reilly might disagree violently: "We have plenty of space. The problem is that the kids are too pampered . . . special rooms for speech correction and reading, plus a swimming pool, plus a gym for boys and another for girls. Why, in my day, one gym served both boys and girls; we simply drew heavy curtains down the middle and you had all the privacy you needed. Get rid of all this nonsense and use this wasted space for the extra classrooms we need."

All the makings are here for a lively discussion. And as long as the discussion remains objective, there is no need for you to interfere. The time to step in fast is when the discussion between John and Jack becomes inflexible and emotional, with the other people stubbornly siding with either John or Jack and refusing to see any of the good points of the other's opinion. When this happens simply switch the group away from the topic they're discussing and onto a different one. For example, you could say, "Right now our school budget won't allow us to build a new school or to remodel our current ones. What can we do with the facilities we have?"

Keeping the temperature level down doesn't mean squelching all disagreements ... there is nothing wrong with a lively verbal battle, well slugged out. But you do want to prevent hurt feelings; many people are sensitive and react personally when their ideas are attacked. So by all means stir up the fires of honest opinion and breathe life and excitement into the discussion. But stop short of going too far; put on the brakes when people get too hot.

And move fast to change topics when remarks start to become personal, when they are directed at people rather than issues ... this is a sure sign that the temperature level has reached the danger point.

PREVENTING LOSS OF THE PERSONAL TOUCH

Hasn't this often happened to you ... you're enjoying a lively conversation at a friend's house when you happen to glance at your watch. "Look at the time," you exclaim. "It's way past midnight. We have to get home and rescue the baby sitter."

When you've spent evenings like this, I'm sure you've asked yourself, "What made the time pass so fast?" Good companionship is part of the answer, interesting discussion topics another part, and a good quarterback who knows when to change the topic is a major part of the answer. When a conversation moves smoothly from topic to topic, no one has a chance to become bored. And in this section and the next are presented two techniques good quarterbacks use to help them spot when the time is right to end the old topic and start a new one.

Since you want to involve people in the conversation, you should try to keep them discussing either:

- topics in which they are personally interested

or

- problems which they can personally help to solve

The key word in the above two descriptions is "person-ally." People enjoy conversations where they can become personally involved.

Going back to the school discussion:

> Suppose John remarks, "Our kids have to take too many useless courses. Why study a foreign lan-guage . . . they'll only forget it after a few years."
> Jack disagrees, "Learning another language is a broadening experience for kids. Besides, they'll need it to get into college."
> John snaps back, "I don't see why colleges should require a foreign language as an entrance require-ment."

It's true that a hot and lively debate can grow from these remarks. But note what also can happen . . . one by one the other people in the discussion realize they have no personal control over college entrance requirements. And as they realize this, they start losing interest in the conversation. What's the easiest way to rekindle this interest? Redirect the topic by switching it back to a discussion of the local schools, to local problems which the others can personally help to solve. Do this and you'll not only salvage the conversation, but you'll further build your reputation as a conversationalist.

SENSING THE THINNING OUT PERIOD

After a new topic is introduced, it usually moves forward nicely as everyone becomes involved and contributes to the conversation. But at some point a peak will be reached; from there the conversation will slow down as one person after another runs out of new ideas to contribute . . . the conversa-tion will thin out as the same thoughts and comments are repeated. This is a perfect time to step in and introduce a new topic in order to keep the conversation moving forward. You can even pre-plan what you're going to say. George Reade does this by asking himself, "What's the next logical topic we can discuss when this one wears thin?" Once he has his answer all he has to do is sit back and enjoy the conversation. When it starts to thin out, he introduces the new topic. That's why he has such an on-the-ball reputation.

There is a rule of thumb that'll help you recognize the point where the thinning out begins: the best time to change a topic is after everyone has had a chance to express his most important thoughts, but the discussion still has enough ideas left over to go on a little further. Cut the topic off at this point and conversations you quarterback will never thin out on you.

PREVENTING THE SIX DEADLY
CONVERSATION KILLERS

Simply by using the techniques outlined so far in this chapter, you will be able to create a lively, forward-moving conversation. But there are six deadly killers that can appear in any conversation, no matter how well it is quarterbacked. All six are discussed in the following paragraphs so that you can spot them quickly and squelch them before they kill your conversations.

Overdomination . . .

There's always one person in any conversation who will talk more than the other people. And this isn't always bad . . . in fact, it can be a definite help to you if the other people are quiet by nature. The danger comes when someone talks so much that the others present have little or no chance to speak up and express themselves. Once this happens, over-dominance is present. You stop it quickly before the others lose interest in the conversation with two easy techniques that I've often used:

- interrupt the offender and invite opinions from the others present.
- switch the conversation to a topic where the quieter people have strong knowledge and thus can make an immediate contribution.

Repetition . . .

I'm sure you've been in conversations where the same thoughts were repeated over and over and over again . . . boring, weren't they! Repetition is a sure-fire conversation strangler ... it kills initiative ... it deadens the mind ... it discourages new ideas ... and it causes people to turn off their thinking and fall into mental slumber. When repetition starts, change the topic fast and inject a powerful dose of enthusiasm to reawaken the interest of those present.

The easiest way to inject enthusiasm is to use both your personality and your voice tone. Here's how Arthur May does this. First he acts and feels excited. Second, he lets his voice almost throb with enthusiasm. This combination is almost irresistible ... try it and you'll see the others around you start to come alive as they react to your enthusiasm.

Side conversation groups ...

Sometimes a conversation moves into a topic that doesn't interest all of the people present. When this happens, the uninterested ones often ignore the main discussion and start up a side conversation with some of the others present. As long as these side conversations last only a short time, they serve a useful purpose ... they give participants a chance to get to know each other better or to discuss something that interests them and not the rest of the group. Side conversations become a danger when they threaten to pull the participants away from the rest of the group permanently. Therefore all you need to do is to keep an eye on the side conversations to be sure that the break-away groups reunite with the majority within a fairly short period of time.

Emotion venting ...

People bristle with emotions ... some have positive and healthy ones while others own negative and self-defeating ones ... some control their emotions while others are controlled by them ... in some people emotions ride up to the surface of their personality while others bottle up their emotions and hide them from the outside world. As a conversational quarterback, you want to prevent these ever-present emotions from destroying a conversation.

And one of the easiest ways to do this is to acquire the

knack of spotting emotional comments and learning when they
are getting out of hand. All this takes is a little experience.

For example: during a discussion Bill Bentley sounds off:
"Boy, is my neighbor, John, stupid! After the freezing rain last
week, he didn't throw sand on his sidewalk. As a result, when
my kid passed John's house on the way to school, he fell and
hurt his leg badly. I ought to sue that no-good bum, John."
Think about Bill's attack on John. It's much too violent to be
just a reaction to a slippery sidewalk. There must be something
else affecting his thinking:

- Maybe John is a constant source of annoyance to
  Bill and the sidewalk incident is the "last straw." If
  this is the case, you should be able to quiet Bill
  down by changing the subject.
- Or maybe Bill is annoyed at something else that
  happened to him and he's using the story of John's
  stupidity as an excuse to vent his emotions. If this is
  true, when you change the topic his tensions won't
  fade away . . . they'll persist to the point that his
  negative emotions may start to affect the feelings of
  other people in the conversation.

If you see signs that Bill's emotional outburst is rubbing
someone the wrong way . . . that it is moving the conversation
in a negative direction . . . then you should take corrective
action. Here are three techniques that have worked for me in
such a situation:

- You can decrease Bill's effect on the group either by
  changing the topic to one where Bill will react more
  objectively or to one where he lacks sufficient
  knowledge to make much of a contribution. When
  changing the topic, you'll always find it helpful to
  do it in a way that opens up the discussion to
  everyone present. For example, "Did you fellows
  read about the new swimming pool the city council
  is planning to build over on East Street?"
- There is always a chance that Bill may not be aware

that he's being too emotional. If this is the case, and Bill is an objective and open-minded person, you can alert him to his emotional outburst with a statement such as "Didn't realize you felt so strongly about this, Bill. We can talk some more about it later. But for now, let's chat about something more pleasant."

- As a final resort, you can try to isolate Bill from the rest of the group for a while. For example, if you're throwing a party at your house, you could ask, "Bill, can you give me a hand for a minute. I think we need some more food and drink, and I just don't have enough hands to handle all these glasses." This will give Bill a chance to do something constructive, and will give you an opportunity to get his mind off the previous subject.

If Bill's influence on the group is not negative, the best way to relax him is to let him continue venting his emotions . . . once they are spent, he'll relax. A few soothing words and sympathetic understanding from you will be a great help to him and will surely win his goodwill towards you.

Emotion dripping . . .

Sometimes sentiment creeps into a conversation, especially when old friends gather for a reunion. And there is nothing wrong with a moderate dose of sentiment . . . it can warm the heart and leave everyone with a pleasant aftertaste at the end of the conversation.

The danger comes from too much sentiment. Then the conversation becomes overloaded with tugs at the heartstrings . . . the participants feel drained and emotionally let down . . . they leave the conversation with an unpleasant aftertaste.

When you see the warm glow of sentiment grow into the dangerous blaze of sentimentality, move in quickly and smother the topic. You can be gentle and use tact, but move quickly enough to be sure that the conversation doesn't become unpleasant for anyone.

Self-building . . .

Some people seem to have only one word in their vocabulary . . . "I." You know the type . . . they're always busy telling everyone how wonderful they are. This self-building takes many forms; the three most common ones are these:

- The offender may talk on and on about all the problems he has. What this fellow is really saying is this: "Feel sorry for me. Listen to what a tough life I lead." If his monologue ends by his overcoming his problems, he is saying: "You know I really am quite a person. I can lick whatever life throws at me."

- Or the offender may fill your head with a long list of the jobs he has successfully completed, and he'll be sure to tell you how hard he worked on these jobs. This person is saying, "Please admire me because I work so hard and do so much."

- Or self-building can even be done without saying a word . . . what the offender does is yawn constantly, look tired and worn out, and keep rubbing his eyes as if they ached . . . there are countless little quiet ways this type of fellow can ask for your sympathy.

Example after example could be given, all illustrating how self-builders try to impress you with how clever they are, how good a job they can do, and how important they are.

A certain amount of self-building is normal and healthy, and you can handle it easily by listening politely and by subtly letting the other fellow know you get his message by commenting:

"That was certainly a good job you did."
"Say, I never realized it took so much work to do that job."

The conversation killer to watch for is the person who carries his self-building to an extreme.

- Put an excessive self-builder with a group of more

humble people and he soon dominates the conversation to the point that the others haven't a chance to say anything.

- Put a group of excessive self-builders together and all you hear is a loud hum of many voices all sounding off at once ... this isn't conversation, it's time-wasting noise.

I asked George Reade what he does when he runs into an excessive self-builder: "I keep the conversation centered on topics where he will not have much of a chance to speak up," George answered. "I know this won't make him happy, but it is far better to have one person not fully enjoying the conversation than to have all the others dissatisfied and bored." No wonder George is so readily accepted in group conversations ... his advice makes a lot of sense.

SEEKING THE "WHAT" AND NOT THE "WHO"

Once a topic has taken hold and everyone is involved in the conversation, comments fly back and forth as people react to the topic. Sooner or later these reactions jell into opinions.

"I think our school needs a better sports and recreation program."

"I disagree. There's already too much energy wasted on athletics. What we need is a better music program."

Since you have been quarterbacking this conversation, its only natural that the others may turn to you and ask, "Don't you agree with us?" This puts you right in the middle. And most of the time you shouldn't agree with either side! Rather you should keep the others talking by giving an answer such as, "How many hours a week do you think the kids should spend on athletics? Or on music?"

You can do your best job as a conversation quarterback by remaining neutral. You want to give the conversation direction and you can't do this if you take sides.

However, there will be times when you feel you have to express an opinion. When this happens, think carefully and before speaking ask yourself, "What is right?," not "*Who* is right?"

During the Civil War, Abe Lincoln was asked whether he thought God was on his side. Lincoln replied that God was on the side of the right and, hopefully, so was the Union. Fortunately, none of us faces problems as grave as those that troubled Lincoln. But we can learn from what he said: If you must form an opinion, then be on the side of the right . . . form your opinion around the facts and not personalities . . . be more concerned with what is right and less concerned with who holds what opinion.

PULLING THE DISCUSSION
BACK ONTO ITS TRACK

There are many topics on which conversations can be built, but there are only two basic types of conversations.

- A social conversation where your only purpose is to entertain the others present.
- An action-oriented conversation where you want to achieve a definite goal.

Handling social conversations . . .

You'll have no problem quarterbacking a social conversation as long as you use the techniques discussed earlier in this chapter. They'll help you prevent the wrong things from happening. Do this and the other people will relax, enjoy themselves and your reputation as a fine conversationalist will be assured.

Handling action-oriented conversations . . .

These discussions should give you no trouble either. The main thing you'll want to do is to keep them on the right course. For example:

- If you start out discussing with your employees about how to improve your department's productivity, don't let the conversation become sidetracked into discussing personal gripes against the company.

- If you start out discussing how to improve your school system's recreational program, don't let the people end up talking about the sports they used to play in high school.

Deciding what goal you want to set for a conversation and assuring that you reach this goal are the subjects of the next chapter, so we won't go into it now.

But before you turn to Chapter 11, review the techniques you learned in these last two chapters ... they're easy to use. And after you've tried them once or twice you'll find yourself using them without even thinking. As your quarterbacking ability becomes second-nature, you'll always find the welcome mat out whenever you join a group in conversation.

11
Taking a Sharpshooter's Aim at a Pay-Off Target

As we discussed in the previous chapter, you'll often enjoy social conversations where your only objective is to relax.

Other times you'll engage in action-oriented conversations. These times you'll want to take a sharpshooter's aim at a target and be sure that the conversation pays off.

HOW TO ZERO IN ON THE RIGHT TARGET

All through your life, you've set targets or goals for yourself:

> **"To become a better conversationalist by learning how to listen better."**
> **"To develop better conversational timing instincts."**
> **"To build a broad and deep knowledge reservoir."**

Target-picking is a vital part of conversation. It helps you spend your conversation wisely by keeping you aware of what your conversation should accomplish. And it helps build your reputation as a conversationalist. When you aim at a target you give a sense of direction to your discussions; thus your conversations are not merely time-killers . . . they accomplish something. They are productive . . . they pay off. And since people feel personally rewarded when they accomplish something, they'll enjoy talking with you.

The kind of targets you should aim at in your conversations range from social ones to action ones. Some common examples are the following:

> **"To help Sally relax and enjoy talking with me."**
> **"To entertain John and Mary when they visit us**

tonight."

"To introduce myself to the new fellow on the job, and to make him feel at ease."

"To renew an old friendship with someone I haven't seen for a long time."

"To learn how to keep my front lawn from browning out in mid-summer."

"To let Joe know about a newly-found vacation spot that he'd also enjoy."

"To teach Ira how to run a calculating machine."

"To convince Charley that it's to his advantage to be more friendly with his co-workers."

All these are worthwhile targets since they give direction to your conversation and help you decide what you want to accomplish.

PINPOINTING YOUR TARGET IN SPECIFIC TERMS

Did you notice that all the previous examples are specific? Each one very clearly defines exactly what you want the conversation to accomplish.

Compare the examples to the target, "To get to know someone new." This target is too general . . . how well can you get to know a person in one conversation? The way to handle a too-general target like this is to turn it into specific targets for a series of conversations. Let's assume that you want to get to know Mike Reynolds. Your first conversation could set the specific target: "Introduce myself to Mike and show him that I'd like to get to know him better." The second conversation could have the target: "To learn what Mike's general personality is like." The third: "To learn what Mike's major interests or hobbies are." By having specific targets, each conversation builds on the previous one until you finally develop a good insight into Mike as a person. You can make many new friends by following this three-step approach.

TAKING THE MEASURE OF YOUR TARGET

No sharpshooter should aim at a target unless he has a way

of measuring how close his shot comes to the bullseye. And to know whether or not you hit the bullseye, you'll need an answer to the age-old question, "How am I doing?" Everyone needs this question answered . . . baseball and basketball players need to know if their team is winning . . . employees need to know how good a job they're doing . . . conversationalists need to know if their discussion is heading in the right direction.

Everyone can get the answer required: Athletes can glance at the scoreboard and know in an instant if they are hitting the bullseye, and employees have their bosses to tell them. Conversationalists also have ways of keeping score, of learning how well they are conversing with other people. An accomplished conversationalist takes the measure of how well he's moving toward his target by carefully choosing only targets that are practical and measurable in the first place.

This principle is best illustrated by taking another look at the Mike Reynold's example. The first conversation's target is practical . . . you can introduce yourself to Mike and show a sincere interest in him as a person. This gives him the impression that you'd like to get to know him better. You can measure how well you get your message across by making the parting statement, "So long for now, Mike. I hope we have a chance to meet again soon and talk some more." You know you have been successful if Mike replies with a comment such as, "Yes, I'm also looking forward to continuing our conversation."

The second target, "To learn what Mike's general personality is like," is also practical and measurable, especially if you limit the goal simply to classifying Mike into some of the general personality groups that were covered back in Chapter 4, "Short Cuts For Instantly Deciding How To Converse With Any Stranger."

If after the third conversation you can name two or three of Mike's major interests, then you know that you reached your target for that conversation.

So far we've discussed three steps that help you decide what you want a conversation to accomplish . . . first, aim each conversation at a definite target . . . second, be very specific in how you state the target to yourself . . . and third, make sure that your target is practical and measurable.

Now that you're aiming your conversations at worthwhile targets, you'll want to develop ways to instinctively and automatically measure whether you are hitting the target. As we discussed earlier in the chapter, athletes can tell how well they are doing by looking at the scoreboard; employees can listen to their boss. Conversationalists, however, have no one else to keep score for them. But they do have a scoreboard . . . the other people with whom they are talking. By carefully observing and evaluating how others react to what you say, you can get a good idea of how well you are moving toward your conversational target.

How to catch facial signals

Many people have faces that light up as brightly as a scoreboard. For example, look at the other fellow's eyes . . . are they bright and interested or dull and bored? Are his eyebrow muscles contracted downward in concentration, or are they relaxed? Do his eyes have a far-off look as if he were thinking about something you said a few minutes ago? Are his eyes sparkling and happy, or do they appear sad and discouraged? Have they a tired look, thereby warning you to keep your conversation light and casual, or does their wide-awake gleam recommend a lively and fast-moving conversation?

A person's lips also can give you signals . . . are they full and relaxed indicating that your listener is at ease, or are they drawn tightly and thin signalling that he feels tense inside? Do the corners of his lips curve upward in smiling enjoyment, or do they curve downward in frowning disapproval?

What about his overall facial expression . . . does he seem relaxed and ready to listen? Or is his face tight and tense, warning you not to start an involved conversation.

Yes, a person's face often mirrors his inner thoughts and feelings . . . you can use this built-in scoreboard to increase your effectiveness greatly as a conversationalist.

Looking for tell-tale body movements

A few months ago, I was sitting in his living room and conversing with John Michaels; my target was, "To help John relax and to enjoy our visit together." But for business reasons John had trained himself not to let his feelings show on his face, so I needed some other scoreboard. Some time ago I found it: When younger, John was quite an athlete . . . in fact, he still prides himself on his fast reflexes and graceful body movements. Therefore, his body became my scoreboard.

When John first seats himself in the living room, he sits rigidly erect, occupying only about one half of the chair's cushion. This is the first clue: John is keyed-up and tense, so I start the conversation off slow and easy by choosing professional football as the first topic. John's body immediately moves slightly forward, thereby telling me that this topic interests him and he has something he wants to say.

When the football topic starts to wear thin, I switch over to discussing the upcoming local mayoralty election. As soon as this new topic is introduced, John's head rises slightly as his body stiffens and pulls ever so slightly back in the chair. There is something about this topic that bothers him; so I immediately change the topic to a discussion of my recent vacation. John's body relaxes a bit, so I continue the vacation discussion.

Half an hour later, John is sitting back in the chair, completely relaxed. His new-found ease is the result of my being able to "hear" what John's body movements are saying and using this information to guide the conversation into topic areas that are pleasurable to him. No wonder John considers us such good friends; I have found the knack of making him feel comfortable when we are together. You can use this same technique . . . show consideration for the other person as a person, and you'll make him feel at home in your house.

Listening between the lines for hidden meaning

Let's use another example to illustrate this technique: For some time now you have felt that your church's financial program badly needs an overhaul, so you get yourself appointed Chairman of the Finance Committee. You set this as your first major target: "To recruit Sam Jenks to head up the canvass team that personally will visit every church member to request a financial pledge." When you approach Sam and offer him the job, he answers, "I don't know. That's quite a responsibility and I'm not sure I can take it on."

Since Sam didn't answer "yes" or "no," you have to

decide whether Sam's answer really means that he doesn't want the job or that he isn't sure he can handle it. The only way to find out is by listening between the lines . . . in other words, by using all your senses to try to "feel" the real meaning of his answer. Suppose you decide that he isn't sure he can handle the job. Then you might reply, "I wish you would think it over, Sam. I'm sure you could do an outstanding job." You might go on to tell him how his ability to handle detail well and to get along easily with other people makes him a natural choice.

Two days later you telephone Sam and he accepts the job, proving that you had listened between the lines correctly to hear the real meaning behind Sam's answer. Often this ability to listen between the spoken lines is a key factor in giving you the reputation of being an outstanding conversationalist.

USING HIS QUESTIONS TO BRING OUT HIS OBJECTIONS

There will be many times when you want to be sure you know and understand what's bothering the people you're talking with. This is especially true when your conversational target is to sell a new idea. Take a second out from your reading and remember the last time you suggested a new idea to someone else. Odds are that many questions and objections were thrown at you when you first mentioned the new idea:

"Isn't there an easier way?"
"Are you serious?"
"Won't this mean more work for us?"
"What's wrong with the way we do things now?"

Don't discourage these questions . . . welcome them. It's human to resist new ideas at first, so it's only natural that your listeners will search for something wrong with your idea. They'll also want to understand how the new idea will affect them. Questions are the best way they can air their resistance and seek an understanding. So listen carefully to each question and answer it as best you can. In fact, encourage the others to ask questions . . . they'll never buy your idea as long as they have any doubts about it. How successful you are in selling your idea often will depend on how good a job you do in eliciting all resistance so you can deal with it.

USING VOICE TONES AS
EMOTIONAL INDICATORS

How often have you remarked to someone else, "Sounds like you have a cold." Or, "You don't sound too well today. How do you feel?" The human voice usually reflects a person's physical condition. And to the trained listener, it also gives important clues about the feelings and reactions of the speaker as well.

Jack Haines, Harry's boss, wanted to change an aspect of Harry's behavior that was annoying other people in his department. Since Harry was a sensitive and moody person, Jack knew that he must time his remarks very carefully in order to assure a positive response.

On Monday Jack approached Harry and talked casually with him to take a reading on his mood. He noted that his voice was lower and quieter than usual; it had a certain tenseness to it. A quick glance at Harry's fiery eyes confirmed his opinion . . . he was angry and upset about something, so this wasn't the time to discuss his behavior.

On Tuesday and Wednesday Jack noted that Harry's voice was higher pitched than usual; his words flowed forth at a fast pace. Jack's evaluation: Harry is nervous and somewhat upset . . . the timing is wrong again.

Harry's voice was still giving warning signals on Thursday. This time it sounded strained and thin, completely lacking in vibrancy and fullness. The tensions of the last three days were affecting him; his energy was wearing thin.

After reporting in sick on Friday, Harry returned to work the following Monday. His voice was back to normal . . . full-bodied and relaxed with almost a lyrical quality to it. Now the timing was right: Harry seemed in the proper mood to react positively to some friendly hints from his boss on how to improve his relations with his fellow workers. By listening carefully to voice tone, Jack had hit his conversational target.

HOW TO TURN THE THINKING OF OTHERS
TOWARD YOUR TARGET

A person's attitudes make good scoreboards, and the two most productive attitudes to look for are his feelings about the topic being discussed and his opinion of your ability as a conversationalist. Since these attitudes exist inside his mind, you cannot simply see or hear them . . . rather you have to detect them by paying attention to the inner feeling you receive as you talk with him.

I've heard this inner feeling called intuition . . . or people sense . . . or feedback from the subconscious. But whatever name you give it, this feeling can be received by listening to others with all of your senses. Whenever people get together, communication occurs on two levels . . . the first is the words that are spoken out loud . . . the second is the emotions that are quietly felt inside.

Many of the times I've witnessed misunderstanding between two people, it was because one person heard the words that the other said, but failed to catch the feelings transmitted along with his words.

I can remember Jerry Lornager telling how he had to reprimand one of his employees, "George had made a major mistake, so naturally I had to use strong words; but I tried to project respect and liking for him at the same time. Unfortunately George heard only my words and not my feelings . . . he got angry and quit. What hurt was the fact that I had been planning to promote him in just a few weeks."

So when the words you hear disagree with an inner feeling you receive, be on your guard. Something is wrong . . . you may be missing the real meaning of what the other person is saying . . . or the other person may not be saying what he really thinks. Catch his real meaning, and he'll surely look up to you as an "understanding and a good listener."

Some people are just naturally good at sensing attitudes; others seem to lack this ability. I say "seem to lack" because all of us can develop the ability . . . all we need to do is to be alert and use our senses when we talk with other people. If you have never received inner feelings when conversing with others, then simply train yourself to be more alert, for example:

- When talking with a friend ask yourself, "Is he enjoying the conversation or is he bored?"
- When you ask someone for information, notice the way he answers. Then ask yourself, "Is he giving me all the facts or is he telling me only as much as he thinks he should to appear cooperative?"
- When you're trying to sell an idea to somebody, keep asking yourself, "Is he in agreement with what I just said? Does he disagree? Is he undecided?"
- When you are talking with someone and he doesn't seem to be paying much attention to what you are saying, ask yourself, "Is he bored with the topic being discussed? Is he preoccupied with thoughts of his own? Is he tired and not interested in discussing anything now?"

By listening with all your senses continually, you'll gradually start to develop the ability to hear other people on the intuitive or inner-feeling level . . . you'll begin to own the invaluable "people sense" that greatly helps you keep score on how well you're doing in reaching the target of the conversation.

TAKING THE ACTION THAT ASSURES
A WINNING SCORE

As we have discussed, by watching the other fellow's reactions you can tell how well you are conversing. But you want to do more than just keep score . . . you also want to assure your success as a conversationalist by using these observations to help you hit your target. And the key to using observations is . . .

How to ask questions that help you decide what to do next.

If your target is, "To help John Michaels relax and enjoy our visit together," then you want to act on questions such as:

- "Is he interested in the topic being discussed?" If his reactions show that he is, continue the topic. If he isn't, switch the topic fast . . . once he loses interest in the topic, he'll also lose interest in talking with you.

- "What are his personal needs and feelings at the moment?" If he wants to listen quietly, then you do the talking. If he wants to talk, you listen. If he wants to blow off steam, you be sympathetic.

If you are a foreman breaking in a new man and your target is, "To teach Joe how to handle a shipping paper," then you act on a different set of questions:

- "Is he a slow or fast learner." If slow, you carefully tell him what to do, then have him handle three or four shipping papers while you watch him closely. If he learns fast, you work with him on one shipping paper, then let him work on his own and spot check one or two papers later in the day.

- "He says he understands, but does he fully grasp what I'm saying?" There are two ways to get this answer . . . either ask him to repeat what you said in his own words . . . or ask him to do that part of the job you just explained. Whichever way you choose, be sure to congratulate him if he understands. If he is confused, put him at ease by saying, "I'm sorry. I guess I didn't do a good job of explaining what I meant. What you should do is . . ."

If you run into Eric Lornd, an old friend whom you haven't seen for years, you'll surely set the target, "To renew our friendship." As happens when two old friends meet, your first greetings are warm and cordial. Then a feeling of strangeness sets in . . . you've been apart so long that you're out of touch with each other. So you go about re-establishing a friendly feeling by acting on questions like these:

- "Do we still have the same interests?" To find out, talk about the common interests you once shared. Rely heavily on your inner feelings or "people sense" to score how he reacts to the topics you suggest. Whenever he reacts positively, pursue the topic . . . use it to help bring back some of the old feeling of warmth that once flowed between you . . . before you know it, you'll have renewed an old friendship.

- "Have we developed new interests that we can talk about?" Let's face it . . . life is not static; it is constantly changing . . . and we change with it. So tell him what has happened to you since you saw him last. Also ask him what's new in his life. As you converse, search for new areas where you can form common interests. You'll know you have hit the target if at the end of the conversation he states, "It was wonderful running into you. Let's plan to get together real soon." Once new interests are established, you'll not only have renewed a friendship, but strengthened it as well.

How to spot changing conditions.

So far we've been discussing how to satisfy specific targets set for single conversations. But there will be times when you're working toward long-range targets such as, "To keep advancing on the job by sensing what the boss wants from me and giving him those results." To hit this target you constantly must re-evaluate what your boss wants from you. For example, when business is good he'll be most interested in finding ways of making enough products to meet demand. When business is bad, he'll be most concerned with cutting costs.

Most of the time your targets won't be as complicated as this example. But whatever your target . . . long range or single conversation, simple or complicated . . . all your scoring is wasted effort unless you put what you learn to work. Conversational targets are reached only by taking positive and well-directed action. Take this action and you'll become known as a result-oriented conversationalist . . . and this is the type of person who gets ahead in business, forms new friends and adds more excitement to his life.

12
Building Close and Long-Lasting Friendships With Conversation

In today's hectic, running world, most people have a lot of casual acquaintances, but few close friends. "There just isn't enough time to get close to others..." is the standard complaint I hear.

CHOOSING POTENTIAL FRIENDS FROM YOUR ACQUAINTANCES

It's true that the pace of life has stepped up greatly over the last few years. But that's no excuse not to make friends. You know from experience that you can always find time to do those things that are important to you. And most all of us will agree that our family and our friends are the most important factors in our lives. So no matter how busy we are, we should always make time to cement relationships in these areas.

Yet we continue rushing here and there, busily occupied with our everyday tasks. This leaves us with only one alternative... stop our hectic pace for a moment and take inventory. Ask ourselves, "How many really good friends do I have?" In nine out of ten cases, the answer is "Not enough." No one can lead an enjoyable, satisfying and productive life without a minimum of close friends with whom he can relax and be himself.

Think for a minute about one of your current friendships and ask yourself, "How did it come about?" When I asked myself this question, my first answer was, "It just happened. We met each other and got along well right from the start." Then I thought some more and realized that the friendship had started as a casual acquaintance and then had almost automatically moved through a definite series of conversational steps... a series of steps that can help you become friendly with almost anyone you meet.

And the easiest way to learn these simple conversational steps is to use them actively in building a friendship. So right now, stop reading and pick one of your acquaintances with whom you wish to become friendly. In the rest of this chapter you will find many references to "Bill X." Each time you read "Bill X," substitute the name you just chose, and then use the technique being discussed to help you become more friendly with this person.

CREATING THE UNDERSTANDING THAT DRAWS AN ACQUAINTANCE TO YOU

In an earlier chapter you learned how to build a knowledge reservoir by developing a generalist's knowledge of topics that interest your casual acquaintances and by developing in-depth knowledge of topics that help keep conversation lively with your friends. You can use many of these principles and techniques in building your friendship with Bill X. They will help you build a bridge of understanding between you and Bill. And they will help you talk to him on a number of topics ... since friendship, like a pyramid, is built on a broad base. Surely you know many people with whom your conversation is limited to only one or two topics such as sports, business, or the activities of a club you both belong to. But with Bill you'll want no limits on the topics you can discuss, since this is the way conversation flows between two people who have formed a close friendship.

As your first step toward understanding Bill, write on a piece of paper five topics that interest him. From this list pick three topics that you also find interesting and circle them. Using the skills you learned earlier, build a knowledge reservoir for use when conversing with Bill. But don't just stop with these three topics ... they're only your door-openers; they're the areas that can help the first bud of interest blossom into friendship. To help the friendship grow, keep seeking new interest areas that can keep conversation between you and Bill alive and vital. Your other friends can help you do this. As Rod Mircham, a conversationalist with a wealth of friends, once told me, "I always look for new topics to discuss. Whenever I talk to a different friend, I'm automatically learning new facts and being exposed to new ideas. What I learn from Joe, I use to liven up my conversation with Sam. It's a self-building process."

USING CONVERSATION TO GAIN PERSONALITY INSIGHTS

Once you know what interests Bill, you understand the "what" of his personality. Next, look at the "how" . . . how does he approach conversation with other people, what is his conversational style? I have found the following questions very helpful in doing this . . . they help me understand how best to match my conversational style with the other fellow's personality, and thus they ease and quicken the process of building a friendship.

- Is he an outgoing or opinionated type who likes to talk on and on, preferring that I just sit and listen? Or does he prefer that I take the conversational lead?
- Does he think before he talks or as he talks? Rob, for example, likes to think quietly about a subject and then talk only when he is sure he has something worthwhile to say. Fred, on the other hand, likes to talk a subject over before he reaches any opinion . . . he works best when he can bounce his ideas off another person and get their reaction before he firms up his thinking.
- How good a job does he do of making himself understood? Walter, for example, is a whiz at expressing himself clearly . . . when he finishes talking I know exactly what is on his mind. Yet Karl "hems and haws" and has a terrible time making himself clear. When I'm with Karl I often help him get his point across by listening carefully and trying to second-guess what he's thinking. Then I subtly help him put his thoughts into words by using expressions such as "In other words, you feel that . . .," "Oh, I see what you mean . . .," "Say, that's a good idea to . . .".

- Does he like to keep his conversations simple and filled with small talk? Or does he like to really dig in and enjoy a serious, meaty conversation?
- How good a listener is he? Does he concentrate on what you are saying or does his attention often wander off the conversation? If he is easily distracted, you'll want to keep your remarks short, simple and right to the point.

I'm sure you noticed that these questions deal with opposite extremes of personality. If Bill falls between these extremes, you can be sure that he is average in the way he talks and listens. But if the questions uncover any special quirks in his personality, then you'll be aware of them and can take them into account when talking with him. Understanding the "how" of Bill's personality will help you talk in a way that won't clash with his conversational style.

Conversationally meeting him on common ground

When on vacation, you've probably often formed friendships that lasted only as long as you stayed at the vacation place. This has happened to me too, and I've noticed an interesting thing about this type of friendship . . . usually it's with a person who's different enough from me that I wouldn't have sought him out at home. But the friendship sprouted because we met on common ground . . . we both were in a strange place and were looking for an agreeable person to associate with. Thus we shared a mutual interest, even if only for a short period of time.

Short vacation friendships aren't the only kind that sprout from meeting another person on common ground. Your friendship with Bill can grow in much the same way. Think about the people you know who have formed good friendships with each other and then ask yourself, "How many of these friendships are based on a common interest?" Stan and Dick go fishing together . . . Frank and Joe have worked with each other on many different committees in their church . . . Joan and Sally cooperated as Cub Scout Den Mothers for two years . . . the examples are endless, but they all suggest the same conclusion:

When two people have an interest in common and get together often enough, that shared interest usually will cause a close friendship to develop.

So compare your interests with Bill's. Then choose one of his strong interests where you're also enthusiastic. Study up on the interests by reading some magazine articles or even a book. Learn enough about the interest that you can talk about it with an easy familiarity. Do this and you'll be meeting him on common ground and starting a friendship that will lead to many pleasant conversational hours.

However, meeting Bill on common ground doesn't mean you must always agree with him. Yes, you want to share a common interest, but you can have a different viewpoint. For example, Phil and Don are both antique car buffs. They don't own the same types of cars, nor do they agree on which are the best ones to own. And each approaches the hobby differently . . . Phil buys an old car, fixes it up and then sells it; Don has bought two antiques, fixed them up and kept them. Yet despite their different viewpoints, a close friendship has grown between Phil and Don based on their common interest in old cars.

In fact, friendships are often stronger when interests are viewed differently. Consider how you would feel if someone always thought exactly as you did . . . at first you would probably enjoy your discussions, as the warmth of agreement flowed between you and your new friend. But after a while your conversation would become stale and boring, as each of you kept saying the same thing. How much more interesting your conversation would be if you both formed your own opinions and then discussed your different viewpoints. This kind of conversational give-and-take makes your conversations livelier and helps the two of you grow and learn . . . you both will leave a conversation feeling a little richer in knowledge and understanding as a result of having talked together. So in your conversations with Bill, meet him on common ground but never lose your own point of view. This will keep your conversation lively and vital, and thus more interesting to both of you.

THREE TECHNIQUES THAT WIN
HIS GOOD WILL

Remember the last time you listened to a youngster practicing on a piano, clarinet or flute . . . as you followed along with the tune you felt relaxed. Then he would hit a wrong note and you could feel your muscles tense as if you were trying to shrink within yourself to escape from the mistake.

This very human trait of withdrawal can also happen in your relationships with other people. You can be moving along beautifully in building your friendship with Bill, and then without meaning to, you can do or say something that strikes a sour note in Bill's mind. Result: He will shrink within himself and start to withdraw from the friendship you are trying to establish. Obviously you don't want to let this happen, and luckily there are three techniques you can use to prevent it:

How to prevent a clash with Bill's personality . . .

This is easy . . . just keep putting yourself in Bill's shoes and viewing each conversation through his eyes, not yours. Here is another chance to use the questions you worked with earlier in this chapter . . . if he enjoys talking, be a good listener; but if he is quiet and would rather listen, be prepared to do the bulk of the talking . . . if his thinking is clear and sharp, let him think a problem through for himself; but if his thinking is fuzzy, he'll appreciate some subtle aid from you in helping him clarify his thoughts . . . if he enjoys small talk, keep your conversations simple; if he likes to dig deeply into a subject, then put plenty of meat into your conversations. By working with the questions, you'll soon be automatically talking from his point of view and you'll instinctively avoid clashing with his personality.

How to build trust so he'll let down his guard with you . . .

To psychologists it's a known fact that everyone wears a mask . . . as kids do on Halloween, adults slip a covering over their faces and hide behind it. Although kids wear masks for fun, adults use them to hide their true feelings and thoughts from the rest of the world. Once when I discussed this fact with a friend, he remarked, "Maybe people hide their real selves behind a mask because they think the way to get along in this world is to be the kind of person other people want you to be."

Whether or not you agree with my friend, I'm sure you'll admit that you can't become good friends with Bill until he trusts you enough to take off his mask with you. Good friends let down their guard when they are together . . . they trust each other enough to share their worries and fears . . . they feel that they can safely relax and let their human faults show through.

Think for a minute . . . what is the one quality a person must have before you will trust him? Sincerity? Yes, but more. Understanding? Yes, this too, but still more. Able to keep a confidence? Yes, this *must* be present. You wouldn't confide how you really felt about your boss to someone who'd go and tell him, nor would you disclose your weaknesses to someone who'd use them against you. Enough said, the point is clear: To earn Bill's good will, make him feel that he can trust you.

How to prevent competition

You know from long experience that you live in a competitive world . . . as a child you compete for grades in school and as an adult you compete for money, status and recognition. No one needs more competition than he has right now, especially not from his friends.

When you're with Bill be sensitive to his feelings and needs. As conversationalist Lloyd Moritz once told me, "When I am with a friend who wants to talk, I don't compete; I keep quiet and let him talk. When he runs out of words, then I speak up and say what is on my mind. But I don't get too involved in what I'm saying, rather I keep alert to his needs and when I feel that he wants to talk again, I switch back to being a good listener."

Being non-competitive doesn't mean you have to give in to Bill's every whim; no one worth his salt wants a spineless yes-man for a friend. Though you don't have to bend over backwards to please Bill, you do want to show him that you recognize and appreciate his better qualities. So in those areas where he wants to be outstanding, step back and let him have center stage. When you do this for him, chances are he'll do the same for you, thereby making your friendship more fun for both of you.

CREATING A NEW SENSE OF CLOSENESS

The three techniques just discussed build good will by preventing sour notes from creeping into your conversations. Once this good will is present, you can use it to help create a new sense of closeness between you and Bill. You do this by the way you react to his strengths and weaknesses.

Lead to his strengths . . .

When you work on a project and it turns out well, you feel a sense of satisfaction. It's only natural that Bill will react the same way . . . and he'll feel a warmth and closeness towards anyone who helps him achieve success and provides a listening ear so he can boast a bit about this success. You can easily do both of these by conversing in a way that leads to his strengths.

But first you must discover what his strengths are. You do this simply by answering the following questions. If you want to, you can jot down your answers on paper for later reference. Or you can just answer them in your mind.

What type of work does he do for a living?
In order to do his job well, what skills and abilities does he use? Does he work well with his hands, understand mechanical things, organize details well, do a good job of supervising others, and so on.
What are his hobbies?
What abilities and skills does he bring into play when working on his hobbies? If you're writing down your answers, place these under his job-related strengths.
Where has he been successful?
Everyone likes to brag a bit now and then about something he has done. What successes have you heard Bill talk about proudly? In order to achieve these successes, what abilities and skills did Bill

utilize? Add these to the list you are creating.

By now you should have a fairly complete list of Bill's strengths. You next want to use this information in conversations with him in the following ways:

- Subtly suggest to him different ways that he can put these strengths to good use, for example:
  "I hear that our church needs someone to edit the newsletter. With your writing ability, you'd be a natural for the job."
  "The school fair needs some help on its decorating committee. You could have a lot of fun making a central display for them."
- After he takes you up on your suggestion, congratulate him on any success he has in a way that gives him a chance to boast a bit, for example:
  "I just finished reading the latest church newsletter. How did you come up with those great story ideas?"
  "I saw the giant clown you made. How did you manage to get it strong enough to withstand the high wind we had at the fair?"

Close friendships can only develop when both people take an active interest in each other's better qualities. Helping Bill put his strengths to productive use is one sure way to do this.

Help him around his weaknesses. Like every other person, Bill has weak points as well as strong ones. Earlier in this chapter, you used questions to help uncover his strengths; this digging into his personality should have given you a good idea of his weaknesses as well. Funny thing about us human beings . . . we all tend to spot a weakness in someone way before we acknowledge a strength.

There are two major ways you can react once you know where Bill is weak:

- You can help him correct his weak points.
- You can help him avoid situations where his weak points might surface for everyone to see.

Helping someone correct a weakness is a delicate task . . . think back to how you felt the last time another person pointed out one of your faults. Let's face it . . . nobody likes to be told he's doing something wrong. Therefore, you must handle Bill tactfully if you want to correct him without harming the friendship you're trying to establish.

One way to do this is by referring to a third person who has the same fault as Bill: "Isn't it annoying how Alex always clears his throat just before he starts to talk?"

There are many ways you can use to alert Bill to his weakness, but whichever route you choose, keep this one rule in mind: Let him know by your attitude that you think he's man enough to correct his own weakness once it's been pointed out.

There are times when just pointing out a fault to Bill may do no good . . . when his weakness is a basic part of his personality and can't be corrected easily. In this case, you might try to help him avoid situations where his weakness would show.

As an example, let's look at one group that is paid to help others overcome their weaknesses—managers in business organizations. Suppose you are the president of a company that manufactures a highly technical product. You have a manager working for you whose strengths are handling detailed jobs and working with other people; however, he is not strong technically. Another manager has a strong technical grasp of your product and is an excellent business planner. The second man's weakness: He lacks the aggressive drive needed to handle many different and detailed jobs simultaneously. As company president, you'd surely recognize the perfect team that these two men would make: One is fast-acting and intuitive, a good administrator; the other a broad and deep thinker, a technical expert. By allowing the men to work as a team, you offset the weaknesses of one with the strengths of the other. If a problem dealing with the daily workload comes up, the administrator can discuss it with his supervisors and find a solution. On the other hand, if a good customer visits the plant with a product application problem, it's the technical man's turn to take the conversational lead and find a solution.

Just as two men can offset each other's weakness in

business, so too, can two friends automatically offset each other's weakness in conversations... all it takes is a few minutes' thought to spot where you're weak and the other strong, and a willingness to let him take the conversational lead in those areas where he has the greater strength.

HOW TO KEEP THE BONDS
OF FRIENDSHIP STRONG

By this time, your relationship with Bill should be blossoming into a good friendship. Now you want to use the following two techniques to assure that your friendship turns into a lasting one:

Give him a sense of reward . . .

You can bet that Bill prefers to spend his time with someone whose company he enjoys. And one good way to make sure he enjoys being with you is to converse in a way that makes him feel rewarded for having talked to you. Simply by using some of the techniques you learned earlier in this chapter you can give him this sense of reward:

- *First,* go out of your way to develop interests that are similiar to his ... then your conversations will be interesting and enjoyable to him.
- *Second,* act in a way that does not clash with his personality.
- *Third,* create an atmosphere of trust and thereby encourage him to drop his mask and be himself with you.
- *Fourth,* help him put his strengths to good use, and help him avoid situations where his weaknesses may embarrass him.

And you can also use this *fifth* and new technique ... discuss a new fact or piece of information in each conversation so that he leaves feeling he's learned something he didn't know before.

By following these five actions you can be sure that Bill

enjoys conversing with you. In fact, chances are he'll often seek you out simply for the pleasure of talking with you. Once this happens you're ready to apply the final technique in building your friendship with him . . .

Enjoy an alert affinity . . .

In chemistry, it is a known fact that certain elements have a natural affinity for each other . . . put hydrogen and oxygen together and they unite to form water, put sodium and chlorine together and you have salt. This same kind of attraction can exist between you and Bill as long as you remain alert and spot any misunderstandings or problems before they have a chance to disturb your relationship.

These problems can crop up suddenly . . . in a moment of impatience Bill may snap, "What is the matter with you, anyway? I told you last week that I would be busy this Saturday and won't be able to play golf" . . . and feeling tired at the time you may forget to put his feelings ahead of yours and might snap back, "I don't care what you said last week! We planned this golf foursome a month ago, and we can't disappoint the other two fellows. You have to play."

Whether or not this conversation turns into an argument depends on how alert you are in spotting the danger signs of temper and lack of concern for the other fellow. Once you spot these signs you can quickly correct your attitude and within a few moments change the conversation back to a warm and friendly one . . ."I'm sorry! I must have forgotten what you told me last week. I'll call Sam; I'm sure he'll be glad to fill in for you."

By staying alert and spotting problems while they're still young, you can create an affinity between you and Bill that's almost as natural as the water-forming affinity between hydrogen and oxygen.

13

Developing Persuasive Conversation That Makes Others Want to Act

Perhaps the most sought-after job skill today . . . and thus the skill that can earn the most money for you . . . is the ability to make others want to take action. If you're a supervisor you'll be promoted faster if you can motivate your employees to do better work . . . if you're a salesman you'll earn high commissions if you make customers want to buy . . . and if you're a schoolteacher you'll get a job in the best school system if you earn a reputation for making children want to learn.

I don't think this ability is in such demand because only a few people have it . . . I believe anyone can be a successful motivator. It's true that this ability comes naturally to some. But even if you're not one of the naturally gifted ones, there's no reason why you can't easily learn and use the few basic techniques that will make you an instinctive people motivator . . . and the key to making others want to act lies in the conversational skills and knowledge presented in this chapter.

HERE'S THE MODERN WAY TO GET THINGS DONE

As you know, nobody willingly lets others order him around . . . employees won't jump just because a boss commands it . . . nor does a teenager "snap to" simply because his father ordered it. People want to think for themselves. In a climate like this, you have to get things done the modern way . . . by motivating others . . . by making others want to do what you want them to. And the way to get yourself started using this modern conversational technique is first by grasping these few basic principles:

- People do what they do because they feel comfortable acting that way . . . when someone's happy with the way things are, he has no reason to change. But if this same person becomes unhappy with his current state of affairs, then he'll feel uncomfortable.
- People don't like feeling uncomfortable . . . so, when they feel this way, they're open to suggestions that will help them feel happy again.
- When they learn of a new way to behave that removes their discomfort, they'll gladly change their actions. They'll be motivated . . . they'll want to act in the new way.

Now let's see how these principles work in everyday situations:

Suppose you're a supervisor and you have an employee, Johnny Treble, who talks too much. In fact, he enjoys talking so much that he dominates every conversation he's in. During one of his monologues, you observe him from afar and notice that Larry Rhodes walks away from Johnny with a disgusted look on his face. You chat with Larry for a minute, then approach Johnny and remark, "Boy, Larry seems angry about something. Don't know what he meant, but he mumbled something about not being able to get a word in edgewise."

This is bound to make Johnny feel uncomfortable . . . he knows that Larry was just with him, so Larry must be angry about the way he acted.

As soon as you notice Johnny's discomfort, you might follow with a second remark, "You know Larry is a great conversationalist. He really knows how to listen."

If Johnny has any sensitivity at all, he'll catch what you're really saying: the suggestion you put between the lines of your conversation . . . "You'll keep Larry as a friend if you simply talk a little less and listen a little more." And, since Johnny is feeling uncomfortable, he'll want to change his way of acting . . . he'll want to remove his discomfort by being careful not to talk too much in the future.

Though all motivating conversations don't go as smoothly as this one, it does illustrate the modern way to get things done . . . first, make the other fellow feel uncomfortable about his current actions . . . second, show him a new and better way to act that will remove his discomfort . . . third, stand aside and let him change of his own free will. These principles can easily be put to work by following the conversational steps described in the rest of this chapter.

As you use these steps, you'll begin developing the persuasive power that makes your conversations pay off. Perhaps when you first read them, they may seem a bit involved . . . but as you work with them, they'll seem very natural. Before you know it they'll become a habit. This is good . . . the power of your persuasive conversation will grow as you use these steps more and more. And the more often you use them, the better you will become at motivating others; it won't be long before you'll have the most sought-after skill on the job market today . . . the job skill that has earned promotion after promotion for many conversationalists.

THE SECRETS OF GETTING THROUGH TO OTHERS

Do you remember how Boy Scouts are taught to make a fire without using matches? First, they cut a pile of dry wood shavings, then they strike a flint until a spark falls onto the shavings. Finally they blow on the spark until the shavings start to blaze.

Getting through to other people is much like this fire-starting project. First you prepare a "bed" of attention, then you strike a spark and conversationally fan it until it creates a blaze of interest.

Let's continue the comparison between fire starting and conversation . . . a spark will burst into fire when the wood shavings are dry and have not absorbed a lot of dampness . . . similarly a blaze of interest is created when the other person's mind is "dry," when it is not absorbed with its own thoughts or emotions. Here are ways to help you break down the two most common mind absorbers that prevent you from getting the other fellow's attention:

Breaking through preoccupations

If a supervisor is busy planning the production sequence for some rush parts, he won't be interested in listening to his foreman's vacation scheduling problems. But his attention focuses fast if the same foreman bursts into his office exclaiming, "Our turret lathe just broke down . . . our whole production line will have to stop unless you order one of the maintenance men to drop a routine job and fix the lathe fast." Moral of this example: When someone is wrestling with his own problems he won't pay attention to you . . . unless what you have to say is more important than his thoughts.

Another way to penetrate a preoccupied mind is to help the other fellow solve his problem. Say, for example, you walk into Bill's office and notice him studying a map.

> "Planning a trip?" you ask.
> "Yeh, got to drive to Buffalo tomorrow."
> "I made that trip last month and the AAA suggested I go this way," you advise, as your finger traces the fastest route. At this point Bill's mind is free and ready to turn its attention to what you have to say.

Relieving the other person's tensions

When someone's nerves are tied up in knots, his mind will be tied up too. So to get his attention you first must relieve his tensions. Here are two techniques I've found helpful:

- Set an example by keeping yourself relaxed. A quiet, soft voice . . . slow and deliberate movements . . . a calm attentiveness toward his personal needs and feelings . . . actions like these create a relaxed atmosphere in which he can unwind.
- Keep the conversation centered on topics that are safe. Don't discuss a subject that may aggravate or excite him. Do talk about relaxing subjects like his

hobby or his plans for the coming weekend. There's one exception to this technique: if he is emotionally up-tight about something, then it's often best to let him talk it out. Once he's had a chance to vent his emotions, he should quiet down and give you his attention.

Making him feel appreciated . . .

Another time-proven way you can gain someone's attention is to let the other fellow know you appreciate him . . . that you value him as a person. Once he senses this high regard, he'll usually show interest in you and what you have to say. Naturally, your feelings towards him must be sincere . . . you'll lose both his attention and his respect at the slightest hint of falseness. Here are some simple techniques our friend, conversationalist George Reade, uses to make another person feel appreciated and thereby to gain his attention:

- Show consideration for his feelings.
- Don't criticize him or embarrass him in any way.
- Listen attentively and sincerely when he speaks.
- Never dismiss any remarks of his as unimportant . . . when he comments on something, think about it and then respond appropriately.
- Recognize his strong points by deciding which of his personal traits he is most proud of, and by showing him that you recognize these traits by comments such as:

"What a memory. Wish mine were as good."
"How do you keep coming up with such good jokes?"
"Boy, you learn fast."

Preventing him from tuning you out . . .

Attention is an elusive thing; just as soon as you think you have captured it, it can slip away from you. That's why I always keep alert for these warning signs that the other fellow's attention is drifting:

RESTLESSNESS. You know what these signs are like ... he shifts uneasily in his chair ... his hands fidget nervously with a nearby object ... you get an inner feeling that he's itching to jump up and run away from you. These warning signs tell you that either he isn't interested in what you're discussing or you're saying or doing something that is annoying him. To cure his restlessness first decide what is turning him off, and then change either the topic or your conversational style.

REPEATED QUESTIONS If he re-asks questions you've already answered, you know that one of the following is happening:

- His mind is starting to wander since he obviously wasn't paying attention to what you said before. If this is the case, then work on regaining his attention.
- He didn't understand your first answer. If this is so, then re-explain your answer in different words, taking enough time to be sure he understands.
- He disagreed with your first answer. The problem of disagreement is so important that we'll talk more about it later in this chapter.

UNRELATED STATEMENTS. Let's say that your company has invented a new style widget that you think will give you some manufacturing problems. You start to discuss these with Terry when he interrupts, "How can I handle my current work with that broken down lathe I've got?" His remark is completely unrelated to widgets; he isn't ready yet to talk about them. So change the topic ... discuss how Terry can either repair or replace his old lathe ... then once

this problem is off his mind, he'll be willing to turn
his attention toward discussing widgets.

You get through to another person by first clearing his
mind of preoccupations and emotional tensions, next by
making him feel appreciated as a person, and finally by taking
care that he doesn't tune you out. Follow these techniques and
you can open up his mind to what you have to say and thereby
start a productive, motivating conversation.

HOW TO PLANT YOUR TARGET IN HIS MIND

Now that you have captured his attention and interest,
you're ready to take the first step in motivating him into
action ... you can conversationally plant the key idea in his
mind that there is a better way of acting than the way he's
acting now.

For example, let's say that you manage a large department.
One of your employees, Sam, is giving you a problem ... though his work output is good, his work area is always
sloppy. Your target: Motivate him into wanting to keep a clean
work area. Thus, you must plant the idea in his mind that
proper appearance is as important as work output. Here are
three conversational techniques you can use to do this:

Using a long established "idea planter"...

Remember how you learned math and spelling back in
school ... you repeated the principles over and over until they
became part of you. Educators discovered long ago that
repetition is a vital link in the learning process. And since you
want Sam to learn that appearance is important, repetition will
also be one of your main working tools. You won't use
repetition in a nagging way; rather you'll drop subtle hints from
time to time.

When you walk by Sam's work area you could remark,
"Your work area looks unorganized ... having any troubles?"
When he answers, "No troubles. Everything's going fine," you
can close the conversation casually with, "Glad to hear it. I

thought maybe you were too busy solving a problem to have any time for cleanup."

Then about a week later you could remark, "The big boss came to work before starting time today and noticed how messy your work area was. He asked me if you were falling behind in your work." This remark reinforces your original comment and adds the extra impact that the big boss is also concerned about neat appearances.

Guiding his thinking with a teacher's technique

Right after telling him the big boss' remark, you immediately might move into another familiar method used by teachers—the question technique—by asking him, "Why do you think the big boss feels that a messy work area means that something is going wrong?" Don't answer the question for him; make him think it through and decide for himself that workers are often judged on the appearance of their work area, especially by someone who doesn't know the details of the worker's recent performance.

By using questions you are forcing Sam to tell you why it's a good idea to keep a clean work area. This technique is much more to your advantage than lecturing Sam on the virtues of cleanliness. When you lecture, Sam will feel that the idea is being forced on him . . . that he has no say in the matter . . . and he'll end up resenting you. But when you ask questions Sam will feel that he came up with the idea . . . he was the one who said that a messy work area reflects badly on him. You'll have planted your idea in Sam's mind without arousing his resentment.

A salesman's method for assuring that ideas stay planted

Once your question-teaching has led Sam to say that cleanliness is important, then congratulate him for realizing this fact. Use a proven sales technique . . . lead him into thinking that the idea was his in the first place. "Yes, I think you've hit on the answer. The big boss must think that anyone who has a messy work area isn't on top of his job." Keep Sam talking and thinking about this discovery "he made." In this way you'll be using persuasive conversation to plant your idea firmly in his mind . . . you'll be making him aware of a new way of working without getting him angry with you for "forcing" him to change.

TECHNIQUES THAT GAIN ACCEPTANCE FOR YOUR IDEA

Next you want him to accept that the new way of acting is better than what he's doing. This is where the fireworks can begin . . . people don't like to change so they naturally resist new ways of doing things. But as Sam becomes dissatisfied with his current actions, he'll feel an inner conflict . . . this works to your advantage. Since people don't like conflict, they run away from it. And if the idea you conversationally planted removes this conflict, he'll want to accept the idea. So keep talking persuasively about the idea, keep motivating him into acting in the new way. You want him to become so completely involved with the new idea that he finally accepts it as his own and acts on it.

Avoiding false acceptance . . .

Be suspicious if Sam immediately agrees to change his habits and work neatly . . . people just don't accept new ways of acting that fast. Ask yourself, "Is Sam telling me what I want to hear without really meaning what he says?" Many people play the game of false acceptance . . . their reasoning is, "Why let myself in for a lot of unpleasantness? I'll agree to whatever he wants and act as if I've changed for a while. Then when he has forgotten about the incident, I'll go back to my old ways."

Of course, two can play this game. What you do is be sure you don't forget. When you see him start to slide back into his old habits, step in fast and reapply your motivating conversation.

Drawing out his objections . . .

Since you know that people resist new ideas, why not draw this resistance out into the open where you can handle it conversationally in a positive way? Here are two key ways to do this:

- Keep asking questions that encourage him to voice his feelings about the new idea.
- Keep yourself under control and don't argue against his objections or try to prove him wrong.

This positive approach helps you because it keeps him open minded! If you started to attack his objections, the other fellow may correctly think to himself, "Why bother talking; he's not interested in my feelings, he just wants me to agree with him." He'll then withdraw within himself. To prevent this, just take the time to consider each of his remarks. For example, here are some of the objections Sam could raise about your new idea:

Sam: "If I have to keep my work area spotless, I'll never be able to keep up my work output."

You: "That's a point . . . the time you spend in housecleaning is that much less time you have for doing the work itself."

Sam: "I just can't waste time. I'm paid to get the work out, not be a janitor."

You: "You're darned right it takes time. I'm glad you realize that."

Later, after all his objections have been aired, you can counter them with persuasive conversation such as: "Although cleaning up takes time, a neat work area allows you to work more efficiently. I'll bet you can keep your area clean and turn out the work as well. Why not give it a try?"

Deciding if his objections are emotional or logical

As he voices his objections, the key questions to ask yourself are these: "Is he over-reacting to the change I suggested? Is he being too emotional in his resistance? If you answer these questions "no," chances are his objections are logical ones. If you answer "yes," then he is reacting emotionally.

Here are some additional questions that help you spot emotional reactions:

- Is his voice higher pitched than usual? Is it louder? Is he speaking at a faster pace than normal?
- Is he jumping quickly from one objection to another as if he were trying to overpower your idea by the sheer number of things he can find wrong with it?
- Is he stubbornly holding to his previous thinking and refusing even to consider your idea?
- Is he bringing up objections that are unrelated to your idea? Does he seem to be hiding his real objections?

In the example given above, odds are that Sam's first statement is a logical objection . . . note how Sam presents his opinion in a straightforward manner. The second comment, on the other hand, has the outward appearance of an emotional reaction.

How to handle logical objections . . .

The easiest way to counter a logical objection is with facts and common sense. But first be sure that his objection has been brought fully into the open. Going back to Sam's first statement, you might get him to expand on his objection by asking, "It's true that cleaning up takes time, but why do you think that work output would fall if you worked in a neater way?"

If he answers, "Obviously, when I'm cleaning, I'm not producing," you have a perfect chance to help him see his job differently. You could explain first that the amount he produces is dependent on how efficiently he works, not on how much time he spends. Second, you could conversationally point out how a neat work area helps him organize the job better, thus allowing him to work more efficiently. The end result, you could explain, "is both a cleaner work area and a higher output."

How to handle emotional objections . . .

Patience and a listening ear are your two major weapons when you face an emotional objector.

The first thing you should do is encourage him to sound off as much as he wants to. Just listen quietly and sympathetically until the full force of his emotion is spent. As mentioned earlier in this chapter, you can't get through to someone who is emotionally up-tight.

After he quiets down is the time to make him realize that he's taking an unreasonable position. Do this by discussing his comments calmly, not by attacking his objections or accusing him of being emotional. Your chances of success are greater if you can get him to admit to himself that he's being unreasonable.

Back to Sam's second comment, here are some ways you can respond conversationally to his emotional outburst:

- "You feel that we need to hire a janitor to help keep your work area clean! If we did hire one, we'd have to prove that your output would increase enough to cover the extra salary we'd have to pay. Do you think this would happen?"
- "I notice that the other fellows keep their work areas clean . . . is their output lower than yours?"

As you calmly and logically discuss his objections, he will begin to feel uncomfortable . . . he'll begin to see that his objections are not supported by fact. He'll begin to feel a bit foolish and, therefore, will start to change his attitude.

During your motivating conversation, keep projecting a sincere interest in the points he raises, and keep showing respect for him as a person . . . never belittle him or laugh at his statements, rather listen to him with the same honest concern that you'd expect from others if you were the objector.

Finally, as his emotions start to fade, help him move from emotional spoutings to logical objections. Once he reaches the point of logic, your chances of motivating him are much greater.

You conversationally motivate someone when you cause him to accept that a new way of acting is better than his way. And since no one likes to change, he'll resist your idea. Bring this resistance out into the open by getting him to voice his objections, then calmly discuss the merits and demerits of his objections. As you do this, he'll see your idea in its best light . . . you will gradually lead him into accepting your idea.

HOW TO KEEP HIM GOING UNTIL
THE JOB IS FINISHED

Once he has been conversationally motivated to your idea, getting him to change often requires no more effort than simply asking him to take appropriate action. In salesmanship this is called "asking for the order." And as any sales manager can tell you, this is the area where many salesmen fall down . . . they present a beautiful case for their product . . . they show the other fellow what he'll gain from buying the product . . . then they stop.

Returning to the example of your employee, Sam, suppose you had gone through each of the preceding steps. You had cleared his mind of distractions . . . you had planted your target in his mind and handled all objections . . . you had led him into accepting the idea as his own. Yet you still haven't "asked for the order." True, he may have agreed, "I think it's a good idea to clean up my work area." But when? Tomorrow . . . next week . . . next month . . . next year? Human inertia being what it is, if you stop your motivating conversation at this point, he probably won't start cleaning until next year. So ask for the order, "That's a great idea you have, Sam. Why don't you start cleaning first thing tomorrow? Before you know it, you'll be finished and ready to start in on your regular work again."

This conversational step is vital; if you want to motivate someone, you must ask him to take action. Don't just present a case and sit there expecting him to take the initiative. Rather, brace up and simply yet firmly ask the other fellow to do what you want him to do. Only when he responds to your request will you have completed your job of conversationally motivating him to take action.

If he refuses to act, you know that you haven't satisfied all of his objections. So return to the previous step and get him discussing your idea once more. Ask questions that encourage him to bring up any objections he didn't voice earlier. Then handle these new objections in the same way you handled his original ones. Once this is done, again ask him what you want him to do. Chances are that he'll go along with you this time.

Now that you've conversationally motivated him into acting in a new way, everything will go along fine for a while. But then the original enthusiasm you created for the new target may begin to wane . . . you may find him slipping back into his old ways. This is the time to follow through, to keep him motivated by using these proven techniques:

Reminding him of the need for change

This technique is similar to the repetition technique except that you're now doing it after change rather than before it. Your target is to assure that he stays motivated, to keep him convinced that he was right in making the change in the first place. You don't have to comment as often as when you were motivating him to change . . . just speak up every now and then with comments such as:

- "Certainly looks like you're on top of your job."
- "The big boss commented today about the change that's occurred in your work area. He's pleased."

Making him happy about his change

When someone does a good job he likes to be congratulated. It's only human. So handle him the way you'd like to be treated by praising him for changing:

"Certainly have to take my hat off to you—the way you keep your area neat, yet still turn out the work . . ."

Reward him with a compliment every now and then, and you'll keep his motivation fired up and prevent him from slipping back into his old habits.

Keeping your interest active . . .

You'll keep his interest in the change alive by keeping yours alive . . . by reminding him of the need to act differently and by congratulating him on his successful change. Give him the total credit for changing, but make sure he knows you are aware of his accomplishment.

Showing that you're sincerely interested in the other fellow and following the actions described in this chapter will dramatically increase your ability to persuade others of your point of view. And by remaining actively interested in them after you have persuaded them conversationally, you'll not only assure that they stay changed, but you'll also earn their respect and friendship.

14

Making Your Voice Work For Your Success

When you first talk with a stranger, his initial impression of you is greatly influenced by the tone and quality of your voice. To illustrate this principle at work, compare how you feel toward someone whose full, mellow voice radiates fellowship and friendliness and someone whose hard, guttural voice hints at a rough and unfriendly personality.

Even among people who have known you for a long time your tone of voice is important . . . it helps you convey the fine shades of attitudes and feelings that raw words alone can't. An excellent example is this description of Ralph Waldo Emerson: "There is a kind of undertone in that rich baritone of his that sweeps our minds from their foothold into deeper waters with a drift we cannot and would not resist." Yes, the way you use your voice definitely has a powerful effect on your ability and acceptance as a conversationalist.

DISCOVERING THE BASIC KEY
TO A COMMANDING VOICE

The starting point for producing a commanding voice is to properly control the amount and force of air that flows from your lungs.

For example, create a mental picture of a musical comedy star singing some lilting songs from a hit show . . . imagine that he's accompanied by someone playing an accordian. As one group of the accompanist's arm muscles pull his hands apart, his accordian bellows stretch, allowing air to rush in. As different muscles bring his hands together, air is pushed out of the bellows past metallic reeds, thus producing music.

In much the same manner, the singer uses one set of muscles to depress his diaphragm and air rushes into his lungs as they expand. When the singer relaxes his diaphragm muscles, his abdominal muscles react by pushing upward on the diaphragm. Obviously this decreases the open space in his midsection and thus forces air out of his lungs and past his vocal cords, causing them to vibrate and produce voice tone.

Learning how to control your voice tone . . .

Where is your diaphragm? Take a deep breath and yell the word, "Hey." Yell it loud in a grunting and *staccato* manner. The muscular action you feel taking place in your midsection is your diaphragm at work.

Take another deep breath and start humming softly for as long as you can. You can feel how you're consciously controlling the movement of your diaphragm . . . you are using it to force air from your lungs and through your vocal cords in a slow and steady manner.

I've used these yelling-humming exercises to show you how to control two sets of muscles when you converse with others:

- Contract your diaphragm muscles to draw air into your lungs.
- Contract your abdominal muscles to force air out at the proper pressure.

And to converse with a commanding voice tone, simply balance the workings of these two sets of muscles by slowly relaxing your diaphragm muscles so that air isn't forced from your lungs too quickly. In other words, let your diaphragm muscles hold back your abdominal muscles from contracting too quickly. In this way you can easily control the volume and pressure of air that's forced past your vocal cords. You can get a good idea of what I'm describing by trying the soft humming exercise again and timing how long you can hold a continuous humming tone.

Learning how to breathe dynamically . . .

The kind of breathing that produces a commanding voice tone is quite different from normal breathing. Your body needs

an even inflow of air. Conversation requires an inflow of air
that's timed to the strength of your ideas . . . a powerful idea
requires more air since it is stated in long phrases and in a
forceful voice. On the other hand, casual remarks use short
phrases and a quiet voice, and thus require less air. Generally,
proper breathing for good voice tone is easily done if you take
in enough air with each breath. And you do this by breathing
from the mid-section of your body . . . stand sideways in front
of a mirror and pretend that the mirror is an x-ray machine.
Then visualize the relative position and shape of your lungs
within your body. One thing you'll notice is that your lungs are
like a triangle . . . there is more space for them to expand at the
bottom than at the top . . . you take in a much greater volume
of air if you breath with the lower and wider part of the lung
rather then the upper, more narrow part. Still looking in the
mirror, breathe these two ways:

> *The wrong way.* Open your nostrils wide and swell
> your upper chest, while raising your shoulders and
> pulling in your waistline.
> *The right way.* Expand your waistline and slightly lift
> your lower ribs. The upper portion of your chest and
> your shoulders should not move.

Actors and singers who must perform in public night after
night have learned to breathe from their midsection. They have
to . . . it's the only way they can effortlessly inhale the air they
need in order to vocalize properly. But professional voice-users
are not the only ones who've learned to breathe properly.
Watch an athlete after a sporting event . . . his shoulders don't
heave as he replenishes his body's oxygen supply.

So take a tip from the professionals . . . breathe from your
midsection. Once you've mastered this type of breathing you'll
always have the breath you need and you'll find that you'll
develop a commanding voice tone that'll soon become a natural
part of your conversational ability.

HOW TO GIVE YOURSELF
A LIFELONG QUALITY SOUND

Earlier in this chapter, you created a mental picture of a

musical comedy star and his accordian-playing accompanist. Recall how air flows out from both the instrument and the performer. Note that the accordian creates sound by pushing air past metallic reeds and vibrating them. In much the same manner, the singer produces voice tone by pushing air past his vocal cords and causing them to vibrate.

Working your vocal cords properly . . .

Take a deep breath and strain your abdominal muscles hard as if you were lifting a heavy weight. As you lift your imaginary weight, you'll feel some movement in your throat . . . this is your larynx lifting up and pressing against the back of your tongue, thus helping you hold your breath.

Your vocal cords are folds of elastic tissue located inside the larynx along with some muscles that change their position . . . the muscles widely separate the cords when you breathe deeply, partially separate them when you whisper, and bring the cords close together, stretching them taut so they can be vibrated by exhaled air to produce tone when you converse. The quality of this tone is affected by how well your larynx muscles adjust your vocal cords; quality is lessened by anything that interferes with their free and even vibration. Thus the proper working of your vocal cords depends to a large degree on the proper working of your larynx muscles. Yet these muscles act automatically . . . you can't control them. Therefore to improve the quality of your voice all you have to do is keep your larynx muscles relaxed so they work properly.

Learning how to relax your muscles . . .

Unless your body muscles are relaxed, your larynx muscles will not relax. You can see this relationship between your muscles by making a tense, tight muscle in your right arm. Note how your left arm is not completely relaxed; it is tensing up as well.

Let's take this experiment a step further and turn it into an exercise. Stand up straight and start tensing your muscles in your legs, then your midsection, then shoulders and arms, then neck. Contract all your muscles; tense them so hard you can feel your body shaking.

Note how your muscles feel.

Now, start to relax your muscles . . . first the neck, then the shoulders, arms, midsection, legs. Relax them as much as you can.

Note again how your muscles feel. They are now sufficiently contracted to hold your body in a standing position, yet they're relaxed and free from excess tightness. This is what I mean by saying your body muscles should be tension-free. Keep practicing this exercise until you become so familiar with how tension-free muscles feel that you can immediately spot whenever your muscles start to tense.

As mentioned before, the only muscles you need to control consciously for good conversational voice production are your abdominal and diaphragm muscles. Working these muscles has no tensing effect on the larynx. Simply keep all your other body muscles relaxed, and your larynx muscles automatically do a good job of producing the kind of quality sound that'll make you more enjoyable to listen to. This in turn will lead others to seek you out in conversation.

TECHNIQUES THAT PUT ATTRACTIVE RESONANCE INTO ANY VOICE

The tone produced by your vibrating vocal cords is so weak that if it were to travel as is from your body, you would hardly hear it. That's why your body has resonators . . . to amplify the weak tone so that others hear it as a vibrant and full voice.

Good resonance produces a quality sound, whether in a musical instrument or in your body . . . guitars and violins use both sounding board and air column resonators . . . pipe organs and marimbas use many different-sized air column resonators . . . your body uses three air column resonators . . . your pharynx, your mouth and your nasal passages. And you can vary the size and shape of these resonators; you can make them wider or narrower, longer or shorter. You can even change the texture of their walls from hard to soft. Because you can make so many adjustments, you don't need the many different resonators required by a pipe organ or marimba.

Your ability to make so many different resonators is

important because each tone pitch created by your vibrating vocal cords requires a different-sized air column for effective resonance. And it is this resonance that adds attractiveness to your voice . . . that gives it the quality sound you need to be an outstanding conversationalist.

Using your pharynx as a resonator . . .

The throat area in back of your nose and mouth and above the larynx is known as your pharynx. Because this versatile resonator divides into three sections, each section able to adjust on its own, the pharynx is a most important amplifier of your vocal tones. Specifically:

- The section above your larynx can quickly change its length.
- The section in back of your nose can either be shut off from the mouth cavity or can operate as part of this cavity.
- The section in back of your mouth can act in harmony with the first section, with the second, with the mouth, or with all three of them.

Because it has so many possible adjustments, your pharynx greatly affects your voice quality and is a major contributor to the full, mellow tones that can exist in your conversational voice.

Using your nose as a resonator . . .

Rub your tongue against the roof of your mouth . . . you are touching your hard palate; further back in your mouth it becomes your soft palate. When relaxed, your soft palate hangs downward and allows vocal tones to enter your nasal cavity. When tensed, it raises and seals off this cavity.

The opening into your nasal cavity is at its widest when you're sounding *n*, *m*, and *ng*. In addition to giving nasal resonance to these consonants, you also can give some nasal resonance to vowels that come before or follow *m*, *n*, or *ng*. For example, compare the sound of *a* in "man" with *a* in "fad."

Try another example: Hum a lively tune with your mouth closed . . . note the quality of the sound, then pinch your nostrils. The fact that all sound stops proves that the vibrant quality you heard in your voice was caused by nasal resonance. Proper use of this nasal resonance helps build life and liveliness into your conversational voice.

Using your mouth as a resonator . . .

Consider how versatile your mouth is:

- Simply by moving your lips, you can create an exit for vocal tone ranging in size from a slight pinpoint to a surprisingly large area.
- You can change the size of your mouth cavity in any number of ways with your tongue . . . by lengthening it, shortening it, thickening it, etc.
- By moving your lower jaw you also can change the size and shape of your mouth cavity.
- At the rear of your mouth cavity are your pharynx and soft palate, discussed earlier in this chapter.
- The only part of your mouth that can't change its shape or location is your hard palate.

How to tune your resonators . . .

To produce the best possible tone quality, simply relax your throat muscles, your face muscles, your jaw, and your tongue. Once these are relaxed, Mother Nature manipulates your resonators for you . . . and she does it automatically.

Your conversational voice sounds best when it reflects your thoughts and your feelings . . . when it helps project your personality. And when you are relaxed, this happens automatically.

HOW TO BE SURE YOUR VOICE EXPRESSES YOUR IDEAS CLEARLY

"I'm sorry, but I didn't quite hear you. Could you please repeat what you said?" I'm sure you've often asked this question, but which might more accurately be phrased as one of two others:

- "There wasn't a large enough volume of tone coming from your mouth. I couldn't hear the words you said."
- "Your voice tone was loud enough, but your words weren't clear and distinct. Therefore, I couldn't hear what you said."

Although either of these statements may be correct, chances are that the second statement is the one you most often want to make.

There's no excuse for anyone not talking clearly. In fact, this is so important in speech textbooks that the proper way to pronounce consonant and vowel sounds is described in detail. There's no need to go that deeply here . . . it's enough just to remind you that you're a better conversationalist when you pronounce your words clearly and understandably. Here's an easy way to find out how well you do this:

- Ask your spouse or a couple of your friends to listen carefully to your conversation over the next week. Ask them to write down all words that (a) they have to ask you to repeat, and (b) are even slightly mumbled or indistinct.
- Then ask them to circle the letters of each word that were the hardest to understand.
- When the week is over, review the list with your listeners.
- Note which letters are circled most often . . . these are the ones that give you the most trouble and, therefore, are the letters which you should take extra care in pronouncing.
- Finally, ask them if they think your conversation is either mumbling and sluggish, or rapid and jerky. Most pronunciation problems stem from one of these causes.

If these four steps uncover any problems, you can take corrective action . . . you either can wake up and liven up your articulators or slow down their speed and move your articulators more deliberately. Your articulators are those parts of your body that help you pronounce words . . . your tongue, your jaw and your lips.

Chances are the letters most often circled in the lists are consonants. And proper articulation of consonants requires free and relaxed movement of your articulators. So make a point of using your jaw, tongue and lips in a free, relaxed and easy manner. Your target is the clear and distinct articulation of words . . . don't try for cultured pronunciation and don't worry about cleaning up a regional accent you may have. You're doing fine as long as you pronounce words in the way that the dictionary says is correct, and you prevent any accent from twisting letter sounds out of recognizable proportion. The most popular conversationalists are always more concerned with sounding natural and clear than they are with achieving perfection.

LETTING YOUR VOICE SPEAK FOR YOUR PERSONALITY

There's an old bromide that goes something like this: "She was so very beautiful that I couldn't wait until I met her. But then she started talking . . ." And there's a proverbial saying that states, "Better to keep quiet and be thought a fool, than open your mouth and remove all doubt."

No question about it, what you say and how you say it are the twin windows which let the outside world see what you're like inside . . . and sought-after conversationalists make sure these windows reflect a pleasing personality. The "what you say" banks off the strength of your knowledge reservoir. The "how you say it" is determined largely by the tone and quality of your voice.

How the depth of your knowledge reservoir shows in your voice . . .

"I believe I shall never be old enough to speak without embarrassment when I have nothing to talk about." While I haven't done anywhere near the amount of public speaking that

Abraham Lincoln had done when he made this statement, the truth of his remarks often has hit home with me. When I converse with others, I do best when I can talk on a subject where I have a good deal of knowledge.

When you talk from a well-stocked knowledge reservoir, not only do your words have weight, but the quality of your voice has added strength. The English poet Edward Young once stated that "speech ventilates our intellectual fire." Let me add that our voices mirror the intensity . . . or lack of intensity . . . of our intellectual fire. Converse on a subject where you have more than enough knowledge to fuel a strong intellectual fire and your voice will naturally reflect the color and liveliness of your thoughts. Converse on a subject where your knowledge is vague and sparse, and your voice will also naturally project the dull and shallow quality of your thoughts. So if there's any doubt in your mind about the strength of your knowledge, review Chapter 7 on adding breadth and depth to your knowledge reservoir.

How your mastery of your emotions shows in your voice . . .

Just as your voice reflects the depth or shallowness of your thinking, it also mirrors the strength and nature of your feelings. Become excited and your voice thins out and rises in pitch. Should grief overcome you, your pitch falls, loudness decreases, and your voice assumes a somber tone. And if you're young enough to still be courting your lady love, I'm certain your voice often has a soft and tender quality.

Your emotions show so strongly in your voice because they are rarely limited to only one part of your body. If you fear something, for example, your whole body prepares to meet the emergency . . . your breathing speeds up, your pulse quickens, and your muscles tense. With all this happening it's only logical that you won't be able to speak smoothly.

There's no escaping the effect emotion has on your voice . . . and there's no reason to want to escape. Your emotions are a natural and normal part of your life, and they can help you greatly when you want to communicate meaningfully with other people.

The important thing is always to keep your emotions

under control when conversing with others. Go on and get
angry . . . don't be afraid to show joy and happiness . . . be
enthusiastic. But at all times keep control; you should be the
master of your emotions . . . never allow them to become
master of you.

How your attitudes affect your voice . . .

Your attitudes . . . the mental approach you take in your
daily living . . . strongly influence the quality of your voice and
thus your ability as a conversationalist.

Sincerity, for example, adds honesty and genuineness to
any voice. In fact, lack of sincerity is one of the easiest attitudes
for someone else to detect.

Next in importance is that attitude commonly called a
"positive state of mind." Actually a positive state of mind is
more than one attitude . . . it's a combination of many attitudes
that cause your voice to project a "yes" quality that listeners
always find attractive.

One final note . . . good conversationalists approach life
from an active point of view . . . they realize that the joys of
life belong to those who shed their inhibitions . . . to those who
react to life's situations in an active and positive manner.